The unauthorized reproduction or distribution of a copyrighted work is illegal. Criminal copyright infringement, including infringement without monetary gain, is investigated by the FBI and is punishable by fines and federal imprisonment.

Please purchase only authorized editions and do not participate in or encourage, the piracy of copyrighted material. Your support of author's rights is appreciated.

This book is a work of fiction. Names, characters, places and incidents are the products of the author's imagination or used fictitiously. Any resemblance to actual events, locales or persons, living or dead is entirely coincidental.

Contract: Masters of the Savoy copyrighted 2022 by Delta James

---

Cover Design: Dar Albert of Wicked Smart Designs

Editing: Michele Chiappetta of Three Point Author Services

Want FREE books from Delta James?

Go to https://www.subscribepage.com/VIPlist22019 to sign up for Delta James' newsletter and receive a copy of *Harvest* along with several other free stories. In addition to the free stories you will also get access to bonus stories, sales, giveaways and news of new releases.

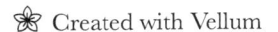

❀ Created with Vellum

CONTRACT: MASTERS OF THE SAVOY

A SUPERNATURAL MYSTERY AND ROMANCE

DELTA JAMES

ACKNOWLEDGEMENTS: *These things are so hard to write. It can't be as long as the book, but you fear leaving people out. So instead, I'll just go with the basics:*
- *To my father who gave me the gift of storytelling*
- *To Renee and Chris, without whom none of what I do would be possible*
- *To the Girls: Goody, Katy, Emma, Roz, Ava and Skylar*
- *To my ARC, Critical Reader and Focus Groups, JT Farrell and all of my readers – thank you from the bottom of my heart*
- *To Michele Chiappetta of Three Point Author Services, Editor Extraordinaire for all her hard work and putting up with my crazy schedule*
- *To Dar Albert of Wicked Smart Designs, the genius behind my covers who works with nothing from me and produces the most amazing artwork, which then become my covers*

CHAPTER 1

Three Months Ago
The Savoy Hotel
London, England

How the hell had everything gone so wrong? It was supposed to be so simple.

Saoirse Madigan was supposed to keep Gabriel Watson, the chief of security, and Felix Spenser, the head concierge, busy at dinner while her friends—Rachel, Sage and Anne—tried to extricate a small cache of jewels and coins Anne had left hidden in the floor of Cardinal Wolsey's wine cellar back in the time of the Tudors. It was supposed to have been a double date—Anne, Watson, Spenser and herself—but the opportunity to get to the treasure tonight had opened up and they'd taken it, leaving Saoirse to distract Watson and Spenser.

She shook her head, internally still wrapping her

brain around the fact that Anne had once been Henry VIII's second queen, Anne Boleyn. Even though Anne had once lived in the sixteenth century, that was nothing compared to the fact that Rachel and Sage had taken the term 'book boyfriend' to a whole new level. All three men—Roark, Spenser and Holmes—had just a year before existed only within the pages of Sage's romance novels. Saoirse smiled as she thought about it. It was completely insane, and yet absolutely true. The best part was amongst the four women, she was the most normal—and she was a witch!

As they left the restaurant, Saoirse cursed her friends. Well, not really, because as a witch she could do that, and she didn't mean them any harm. But she couldn't help wondering how she'd gotten herself into this mess, and more importantly, how to extricate herself from it before it blew up in her face. She had to ask herself, so what if it did? It wasn't like it would have any impact on her friendship with Rachel, Sage and Anne. What was it exactly she feared losing?

Her friends were risking little beyond nursing an aching backside in the morning. Sage and Roark were married, and Rachel was engaged to Holmes. Both couples lived a D/s lifestyle. So while their male counterparts might not look too kindly on them getting up to something dangerous after dark, the consequences weren't something that either woman didn't enjoy to a certain extent and accept.

Watson might be enamored with Anne, but he

knew nothing about her origins or who she was except what little the men had been told. Even so, he seemed to get highly aroused, territorial and possessive whenever he was around her. It had taken a king and his whole privy council to bring her down before. Gabriel Watson didn't stand a chance of winning Anne's affections, much less her submission. Not unless Anne was enamored of the whole lifestyle and could embrace it as her own.

Saoirse knew that both Holmes and Spenser—she rather preferred that to Felix—were members at Baker Street, the celebrated lifestyle club in London. She had been invited to come as a guest a couple of times but had demurred. It wasn't that she judged her friends; it was simply that she had traveled that road once before with a man she had trusted. To say it had ended badly would be putting it mildly. She'd tried giving over to a man who she thought she would build a glorious life with, yet it had been a dismal failure. Turned out he needed her financial stability while he built a whole different life with one of his, for lack of a better term, groupies.

Saoirse had sworn never to indulge that side of her personality again. Being a witch was all about empowerment, and she'd never seen anything empowering about submitting to anyone other than herself.

Holmes and Spenser had managed to escape the pages of Sage's books before Roark, but all three were now firmly entrenched in this reality with no desire to return. They had a friend, Eddy, who remained behind the Veil with no desire to enter this existence, but was still able to communicate with and help his friends.

She'd tried telling herself she was keeping Watson and Spense distracted so that her friends could accomplish their mission, but she didn't want to lie to herself either. For a casual gathering of friends, as opposed to a double date, she'd gone to an awful lot of trouble—a new dress, sultry makeup with smoky eyes and stupid heels. She looked far more respectable to walk into the Savoy Grille than her usual bohemian garb with flat-heeled boots. Still, she was helping her friends, not trying to entice or attract Spense, which was never going to happen. Saoirse believed that Spense seemed mildly indulgent of her being a witch —he didn't really believe but was much too polite to tell her he thought she was crackers.

It had been difficult to ignore the images that leapt to mind when she closed her eyes and allowed herself to fantasize what being with Spense might entail. The whole situation had become a conundrum, which made her somewhat anxious at dinner. She sensed Gabe wasn't buying any of it. He kept the conversation coming back to Anne not feeling well, which meant she had to redirect it, which meant she couldn't just relax and have a good time.

Saoirse suddenly realized Gabe had been talking

and she hadn't been paying attention. She really needed not to do that. Gabe was far too astute to merely ignore. He wasn't a man who would be easily redirected, but she was far more interested in encouraging Spense's attention than she was in making sure none of the men in their little group found out what Sage, Rachel and Anne were up to.

"Exactly what is it you don't want me to find out upstairs?" Gabe asked.

"What? I'm not sure I know what you mean," answered Saoirse, trying to cover the fact that she didn't want him to go upstairs and that she had been too much inside her own head to hide it.

"The hell you don't. What are Rachel, Sage and Anne up to?"

"Gabriel, you have no reason to think that Saoirse has been less than truthful," said Spense. He so quickly stepped up to defend her, she almost felt guilty.

Saoirse was pretty damn sure Gabe knew they were trying to pull the wool over his and Spenser's eyes. Spense wouldn't necessarily think that because he was a nice guy and tended to believe what people told him. Especially people he trusted... like her. She winced internally. That hurt more than just a bit.

The fact was, she found Spense wildly attractive but knew he could never see her that way. Saoirse believed he saw her merely as some kind of exotic, Irish bohemian. Oh, he might imagine her when he was thinking about romantic partners in the abstract, but it took more than attraction to make a relationship work in the real world. On the other hand, Saoirse could easily envision him naked and driving hard up into her body as she clawed at his back and cried out his name.

Wait! What was Gabe saying? I have to get a grip and pay attention, or my friends might end up face down over their partners' knees.

What the hell was happening? Suddenly Gabe was pushing away from the table and standing up. What was she going to do now? Sage really should have been the one to stay. She was far better at making up stories than Saoirse.

Shit! Why did the idea of being face down over a man's knee suddenly make all her feminine parts tingle in a way they hadn't in a very, very long time? Why was she suddenly able to envision that kind of scenario with Spenser? She supposed it could be rooted in a brief conversation she'd had with Gabe the last time she visited the Savoy.

They were the only two occupants on the elevator that day.

"You and Felix ever going to quit dancing around each other?" Gabe asked out of the blue.

The question caught her off guard. "Felix? I'm surprised he even lets me in his hotel. I'm really not the sort he wants to encourage as clientele."

Gabe eyed her carefully. "You'd be surprised," he

mused. "Felix is the most non-judgmental person you'll ever meet. He's the Dom at the club they give the true brats to. He doesn't react to them the way most Doms would, and he trains them to his hand pretty easily. Don't let the gentlemanly ways fool you. Felix Spenser can be one tough sonofabitch if the situation calls for it."

"He's a Dom? I can see you and Roark, but Felix?"

Gabe chuckled. "Doms come in all shapes, sizes and skills. We aren't interchangeable, and the club tries to match the right sub to the right training Dom. The subs Felix trains adore him and are highly sought after at Baker Street."

Saoirse shook her head. "He doesn't see me that way…"

"Tell yourself that if you want to, but you're not fooling anyone else. I think you'd find the Gentleman Dom is more than a match for some of your more notorious behavior. I'd love to see the two of you tangle at the club."

"Don't hold your breath, Watson. I'm not geared that way."

As the door to the elevator opened, Watson grinned at her. "Don't ever say I didn't give you fair warning."

Saoirse had been caught so off guard, the doors had closed in her face before she could react.

Now, she was caught off guard again. Their plan

had run amok. Gabe was able to see through their ruse. She probably should have cast a spell that would have kept him in the dark, but she didn't do magick lightly and she sure as hell didn't use it against a friend. Now, he was intent on heading up to Anne's room—technically her room—while he handed her over to Spenser, whose firm grasp wasn't painful in the least.

Nor was it something she could escape easily, as she discovered when she tried unsuccessfully to squirm free.

"So, Saoirse, what are they up to?" Gabe pressed.

"I'm pleading the Fifth," she countered.

"They don't have the Fifth Amendment here in Britain."

"Nothing is going on, Gabe," she insisted.

"All right. Then you stay here with Felix, and I'll go take the girls some chocolates. Women crave chocolate when they're on their period, right?"

"Some women like salt," said Saoirse, trying to think of something, anything, that could keep him away from the room she and Anne were sharing.

"Fine. I'll take her some potato chips as well."

"Why don't I just call up to check on them?" she offered.

"Felix, why don't you take Saoirse into my office and keep her there until I give you the all-clear?" countered Gabe, who was clearly not about to be deterred.

"Do you really think there's trouble?" Felix asked, his fingers closing more tightly around Saoirse's wrist, holding her gently in place.

"Trouble, as in they'll get themselves hurt?" Gabe asked. "Doubtful. Trouble, as in doing something they shouldn't be? I'll bet you lunch on that one."

Felix looked at Saoirse in a way she'd never seen him do before—as if he was reassessing her and coming to a different conclusion.

"I don't think I'd win that bet. Would I, Saoirse?" She said nothing. "That's what I thought. Saoirse and I will wait in your office for your call." Felix stood, moving his grasp from her wrist to her hand and helped Saoirse to her feet.

Saoirse was shocked, intrigued and aroused by the change that seemed to come over Felix. She could feel color staining her cheeks, and her eyes widened. She hoped like hell both men missed her reaction. Felix might, but she doubted Gabe would. The ever-widening grin on Gabe's face did not bode well for her.

Felix said nothing, simply nodded as he led her toward Gabe's office. She could see Gabe heading toward the bank of elevators. She had to do something.

"I don't think he should intrude if Anne isn't feeling well," she offered as she tried to pull away from Felix. His grip remained gentle but persistent.

"And I'm beginning to suspect my friend Gabriel

sees things more clearly than I. If he proves right about Anne, Rachel and Sage, he may well be correct in his observations about you and that you are in desperate need of a dominant partner."

That got her attention. "A what?"

But before she could say anything else, she spied Roark and Holmes entering the lobby. The plan had gone from running amok to full on clusterfuck. If Anne, Sage and Rachel hadn't made it back or if any of the men found out what they'd been doing, there would be hell to pay. Not that they wouldn't be supportive if they knew the whole truth. But it was Anne's secret to share, and she was even less trusting of men than Saoirse, which was saying a lot. Explanations would need to be made and Anne was not yet willing to make them.

Saoirse tried to follow the three men to the elevator but was prevented from doing so as Felix pulled her close. The tensile strength in the man was just now registering with her. She wasn't going anywhere the head concierge didn't want her to go.

"I see them too," he said calmly. "If your friends are up to some bit of mischief, they are about to be found out. I think you and I should go talk about the consequences they will be facing—the same kind you should be facing."

"Consequences? What the hell are you talking about?" Saoirse snarled.

Felix said nothing as he ushered her past the front

desk and into Gabe's private office, closing the door behind them.

"Yes, consequences—as in discipline. I suspect you could do with a good dose of it as well."

"You want to tell me what's going on, Felix?" she asked, pulling her arm loose. He blocked the door, looking annoyed.

"Are they even up there?" he asked.

"Are you calling me a liar?"

Felix shook his head. "Not the best way to handle this, Saoirse—not for you or your friends. I think that perhaps Gabe was reading the situation more clearly than I. Anne wasn't feeling badly, was she? The three of them are up to some mischief the four of you don't want Holmes, Watson or Roark to find out about, aren't they?"

It was as if she was standing with a stranger. The sweet, kind man she'd known since getting involved with Rachel's friends seemed to have transformed into something more—something that called to a place she'd long ago tamped down into the deepest, darkest part of her. Something she had vowed never to allow to return to the light of day.

CHAPTER 2

Without a doubt, Saoirse was the most stunning woman Spenser had ever laid eyes on. Not conventionally beautiful like the models on the magazine covers, but she shone in her own unique way—much like her friends Anne, Sage and Rachel. While Anne might not be wearing Gabriel Watson's ring or even his collar, he didn't know anyone who thought of her as unattached. While Gabe might not have made his intentions formal, he'd certainly made them known.

Gabe and Spenser had talked about Saoirse on numerous occasions. At first, anytime the hunky head of security brought up her name, Spenser had experienced anger and frustration. Gabe had noticed and reassured him that while he, too, found Saoirse attractive, he didn't feel they were a good match. He was, however, quite supportive of Spenser pursuing something with the beautiful, tempestuous witch. Initially, he had dismissed the notion out of hand, but as time went by, he'd found himself concluding that he had been a fool, and that he might be just the man who could provide her with the structure and support she most desperately needed.

Spenser knew Saoirse was a bit eccentric, being a witch and all, but he found her enchanting and gorgeous. What Saoirse really needed was a man who cared for her, put her needs first, kept her safe, and provided her with what she needed, not just what she wanted. In short, the beautiful Irish witch needed a Dom, although according to Saoirse's friend Rachel, she had no interest in the lifestyle. Spenser had smiled to himself. He'd often found that the subs who needed the most dominance were the ones who caterwauled the loudest about neither wanting nor needing it. He took great pride and satisfaction in taking an unhappy, protesting sub and turning her into the proverbial kitten who purred when her master stroked her.

Since he, Roark and Holmes had left the pages of Sage's romance novels, he and Holmes had become members of and frequent visitors to Baker Street. Sage had written Roark and Holmes as very dominant men; she had written Spense as a kind of foil to their personalities. She had also written him as a homage to *Hercule Poirot*. Sage had been surprised when he had appeared in the flesh, looking nothing at all like her description of his character, and shocked when she'd seen the quiet dominance of his personality.

Spenser prided himself on being more of a gentleman Dom—not quite as tough as Holmes or Roark, but every bit as strong. He'd come out of the book with elegant manners and a more refined style in everything he did. Like Holmes, he was quite popular with the subs at Baker Street, making him one of the go-to training Doms for especially fractious subs. They found his quiet, gentle style gave them nothing to rail at, and he could be quite strict if the occasion called for it. More than once, he had been a sub's last chance to remain a member of Baker Street. Spenser had found great satisfaction in that role.

Although he was more than capable of handling one, he'd never cared for brats—well, not until he'd met Saoirse Madigan. He normally took his subs in hand with a quiet authority to which they responded positively. He delivered discipline in a skilled and experienced manner; it was something he enjoyed providing for them. He had enjoyed pleasuring them and being pleasured in return.

Spenser had never thought in terms of a long-term, committed relationship—not until he'd seen both Roark and Holmes find that kind of happily-ever-after for themselves. Now, whenever he watched his friends, he knew there was something missing in his life. He'd discovered that something was Saoirse, but he had doubted they could find common ground. Both Holmes and Watson had suggested that Spenser ought to rethink that.

Every time Saoirse came to the hotel, he found his senses were on high alert. In fact, he was so acutely aware of her presence that he generally became uncomfortably hard whenever he was around her. Something about her arrogance, tempered by a good heart and a sweet nature, enticed him and made him feel protective. He knew from Rachel that she had been married, and that the marriage had ended in a nasty divorce. And it was clear someone had hurt and disillusioned her badly. Spenser not only wanted to heal that wound but pummel the man who had done it.

He wondered if Holmes might be right. Could he tame this beautiful woman to his hand—this gorgeous, eccentric, brave, charismatic witch? The mere possibility made his cock ache.

Still, it could all go very badly. Chancing it could ruin the friendship they seemed to be developing, which could make their close circle of friends uncomfortable. Saoirse had never indicated she was looking for a romantic partner, much less a Dom. He wondered if she'd ever truly submitted. He rather imagined she could play at being submissive, but did she have the strength required to truly give herself over to a Dom?

He held onto Saoirse as Holmes, Watson and Roark headed upstairs to deal with their ladies, leaving him to deal with the lovely witch. She glared at him.

"Maybe heroines never get menstrual cramps in Sage's books, so you boys just don't know how to handle it."

Her snarky comment brought him back to the problem at hand. If and when she was his sub, she would learn not to turn that sarcastic, snide tone on him.

He shook his head. "Not at all. Just because the three of us only existed in Sage's books before last year does not mean that we were unaware of the things that went on in the real world."

"What was that like—you know, being in the book and then being out?"

Wow, she could change subject and temperament in the blink of an eye! He nearly laughed at her nerve. Seeing that snark hadn't worked, she was now trying to deflect his questioning. God, how he wished he had the right to pull her over his knee and spank her glorious ass until she decided to come clean, but he didn't… at least not yet.

Where the hell had that thought come from? From the same place all his other errant thoughts had come—somewhere below the belt.

Forcing his thoughts to the matter at hand, Felix directed her into a chair and answered her question.

"It was rather odd. We weren't always sentient. Once we were, it was a bit like a man dying of thirst seeing a mirage of an oasis. We knew what we longed for but couldn't quite achieve it. Roark was able to push the boundaries on a number of occasions to be with Sage in her dreams, but it wasn't until the hitman tried to kill her that he was able to break free."

"But weren't you and Holmes already here?"

He nodded. "Yes. The timing is a bit hazy, and the further we get away from it, the more the precise memories seem to fade. As far as any of us can remember, Holmes and I got out of the books about a week before Roark, but we have no idea how it happened. I just woke up in a small room here at the hotel because, as in Sage's last book, my flat was being painted. It was the same way for Holmes—he woke up in his bedroom."

"What did you do?"

Felix smiled. "We called each other. Luckily, we exited the books with our mobiles intact."

"Were you excited?" she said, leaning forward, her eyes wide and her focus intent. "Afraid?"

"Both. It was thrilling and a bit overwhelming to be here. At first, I think we all lived with the fear that somehow we'd be pulled back and would lose everything. That's what kept Holmes and me from trying to make real connections outside of each other and Roark."

"Is that the reason you became members of Baker

Street? Sexual pleasure without commitment of any kind?" When Felix raised his eyebrow, Saoirse shrugged her shoulders. "Rachel and Sage don't make a big deal of it, but it's come up in conversations. They keep telling me I should come with them one night."

"I fear, my sweet Saoirse, you have little understanding of the D/s lifestyle. Would exploring that world be of interest to you?"

"None whatsoever." That was disappointing for him to hear, but then she went on, her voice tight as she explained herself. "I know they both say they found a better part of themselves in submission, but having traveled that road once before, I'm not inclined to go that way again."

So, he was right. She'd been hurt and now she was scared. He rather imagined if he said that to her, she would deny it vehemently. "Rachel mentioned you had an acrimonious divorce. I'm sorry to hear that. I have to say that the marriages I have seen at the club, for the most part, seem incredibly happy and stable."

"She tells me that one of the foundations of the lifestyle is open and honest communication. I don't know if that's true, but I do know that it was not a part of my marriage."

"Did he have a problem with you being a witch?"

She laughed. "No. He fancied himself a pagan priest; he liked to say he was descended from King Arthur. He even had his last name changed legally to

Pendragon after we were divorced. He was and is a putz. I should have seen that long before I caught him fucking another woman in our bed. The day the papers were final, I hauled that thing out to the circle of stones on my farm and burned that sucker." She grinned at him when she saw him smile. "Does it bother you that I'm a witch?"

Felix thought for a moment. It would be far easier to tell her where he'd finally ended up, but she deserved to know what had led him here. More than most, Saoirse needed full disclosure, and giving her what she needed started now.

"I must admit the first time I heard you were a witch, I scoffed at the idea. But after hearing and seeing the things you can do, I would be a fool if I didn't believe. As it seems to be an integral part of who you are, the right romantic partner would not ask you to change a fundamental part of your being. He might impose some rules on the use of your power…"

"Rules? See? Therein, lies the problem. Men don't understand what I can do, but they want to control it or use it for their own ends."

"Let me guess—he wanted you to use your magick for his good, so he didn't have to work at it."

She nodded.

"I find that behavior appalling," said Spenser. "In my opinion, a proper match for you would be someone who supports you and what you do but ensures that you don't use your magick to deceive him or in a way that could endanger you."

Saoirse shook her head at his words. "Most magick is inherently dangerous," she countered. "You lessen the danger by studying and learning, and you don't use it for stupid, material things. That SOB actually wanted me to a manifest a luxury SUV for him."

"Unacceptable."

"Plus, it's not always possible to protect yourself."

He cocked his head, paying close attention. "How so?"

"Sometimes," she said, "like with the Ripper and Rachel, you have to put yourself on the line. What good is being able to do magick if you can't help a good friend?"

Spenser understood. "I would agree with that. There are some things worth risking it all for."

Saoirse looked at him, raising her eyebrow in skepticism. "That sounds fair, open-minded and incredibly supportive."

"I believe that a good Dom is all of those things. Plus, I try not to judge anyone. Having once been only a character in Sage's books, that's a bit like the pot calling the kettle black."

"Is Watson going to be really mad at Anne?"

Saoirse should never play poker, her face showed all of her emotions and the thought process behind them. She'd done something in support of her friends but was now worried they might end up with painful consequences. If they were trying to hide something because they knew the dominant partners in their lives would not have allowed it, Saoirse was right to be concerned.

"If she had you lie to him to keep him from knowing what she was really doing, yes. If Rachel and Sage were in on it and it was either illegal or dangerous, I suspect both of them will be receiving a good dose of discipline over Holmes' and Roark's knees, respectively. And Anne may find her relationship with Gabe moving to a new level, resulting in her receiving the same treatment."

"Watson and Anne don't have a relationship," said Saoirse, frowning.

Spenser chuckled. "They do; it just hasn't been consummated yet. I suspect come morning, that will no longer be true."

"You think he'll spank her?" Saoirse asked.

"If she's been lying to him, most definitely."

"That doesn't seem quite fair," asserted Saoirse.

"Fair? That the three of them are most likely going to be spanked, while you aren't? If you like, I'd be happy to change that for you."

"I'm not your sub or your romantic partner."

"Not at the moment, but the future is rarely static."

That seemed to set her back on her heels. Spenser knew if he pressed, he could not only get his relationship with Saoirse off on the right foot, but it would go a long way to jump-starting it. But it needed to be her choice. When she turned away, he took a step back. She needed time to think. And he was in no hurry. All good things were worth waiting for.

CHAPTER 3

Present Day
Savoy Hotel
London, England

Saoirse Madigan woke to the sound of the ocean and the smell of the sea. She shook her head, trying to dispel the last vestiges of what many would call a dream, but which she knew to be a vision from the past. She wasn't anywhere near the ocean. She was in London, at the Savoy, and later today two of her closest friends, Rachel Moriarty and Anne Hastings, were getting married to two of the most gorgeous men she'd ever seen—Michael Holmes and Gabriel Watson.

Long before Saoirse had known she was a witch, she knew she had the Gift—she could see and feel things others could not. One of the first had been the ghost of a young girl of maybe eight or nine years old, wearing a yellow dress from the Victorian era. Saoirse had been about the same age and many years later guessed that the child had chosen her because they were of a similar age.

For the longest time, the child would simply appear, holding her bonnet in her hand and staring at Saoirse. Saoirse tried speaking to her, but the child didn't respond. As Saoirse grew older and tried to approach the apparition, it would disappear. When she turned fifteen, the child appeared and then turned and walked away as it dissipated into nothing.

Saoirse hadn't seen the little girl for years until the first time she visited her friend Rachel Moriarty, soon to be Holmes, at the Savoy. The first time she'd used the elevator to go up, the little girl had appeared and at the fifth floor, the elevator had stopped briefly, and the child had walked through the closed doors before the car began to rise again and stopped at Rachel's floor.

Curious. She hadn't seen the little girl, whom she had christened Victoria, for many years. Once she had discovered she was a witch, she had tried summoning her, but the child had never answered. Saoirse had not thought to see her again until she had appeared on the elevator with her at the Savoy.

Who is she? Why is she at the Savoy? And what does she want with me?

Saoirse sat up in the bed, swinging her legs over the side and standing up. She glanced toward the window that looked over the Thames. Victoria was standing there, staring at her.

"Hello, Victoria. I haven't seen you in a long time. I'm sorry if that isn't your name, but I've never been able to find out who you are or were," said Saoirse gently.

"They're all here, you know," the little girl said, speaking for the first time in all of their encounters. Saoirse felt a shiver run up her spine.

"Who? Who are all here?"

"All the lost ones," the ghostly girl said. "We've been waiting. I told them some day you would come for us. Some day you would lead us to the Light."

Saoirse felt as though she'd been punched in the gut and plopped back down on the bed. Her recent involvement with Anne and her escape from the Void had left her in no doubt as to where it was 'they' wanted to go.

"I don't know how to help you," Saoirse said.

The little girl turned, cocked her head to the side and said in a sing-song voice:

"They did not search for those who died;
The chapel bell did not knell;
When the Irish witch can answer why,
Then our spirits will arise from Hell
And with the King of Kings we will abide."

The child hesitated a moment, turned away and

then went to the door, passing through it as if it weren't there at all. Why had she appeared today, and what the hell did she mean by that? Saoirse grabbed a pen and piece of paper and copied down what the little girl had said. Staring at the door intently, she was startled when the phone rang.

"Saoirse? It's Felix. Would you like to have breakfast?"

The head concierge of the Savoy was a curious man. The last time she'd been here, the group of friends had fought off the Angel of Death and his cohort to keep them from dragging Anne back beyond the Veil and into eternal darkness. Today, she was here to celebrate two of her closest friends getting married to the men of their dreams. And through it all, she still couldn't quite figure this particular man out.

Saoirse and Spenser had had some interesting conversations, but it seemed they were forever circling each other. That wasn't true—she circled Felix like the proverbial moth to a flame while he waited patiently and watched her spin.

"Just us? I mean, just you and me?"

He chuckled. "Yes. Just the two of us. If you think we need a chaperone, I suppose we could ask Sage and Roark to join us."

"I don't need a chaperone. But would you mind having breakfast in my room? I'd rather only have to worry about getting presentable once today."

"Of course. Are you feeling up to company? If not, I can just have something sent up…"

"No, Spense. Can I call you Spense? Felix just doesn't suit you, in my opinion. I enjoy your company, and I'd like to talk to you about something without worrying we might be overheard."

He chuckled again, sounding mischievous. "Now that *is* intriguing, considering some of the things we've discussed in various public areas. Do you have anything in particular you like from the menu?"

"I love the French toast, but I need some kind of protein…"

"Why don't you let me just have them make us a tray with French toast, eggs, breakfast meats and some other treats?"

"And hot tea…"

"I know, Irish breakfast tea and lots of it."

"You're a good man, Spense, I don't care what the other girls say."

"I'll see you in a few minutes."

Saoirse hung up the phone, stood up and stretched. She grabbed her robe and walked into the bath. Since she didn't have time for a shower, she simply washed her face and brushed her teeth, slipping on the garment when she heard a knock on the door.

She opened it and smiled. Spense. Sage had explained that he was the one character who looked nothing like she'd described him in the book. Instead of being an homage to *Hercule Poirot*, Spense was tall, sleek, lean, and powerfully built, with a small, vertical scar by his left eye. His chestnut hair always tempted her to run her fingers through it to mess it up. He had deep brown eyes and a sensual mouth. There was something about the man that spoke to a place deep inside her. As cheesy as it sounded, everything about him pleased her—his voice, the way he looked, the way he supported his friends, the way he greeted guests—yeah, he did something for her.

"Oooh, this smells good. What did you bring for us to eat?"

"Cinnamon brioche toast, thick-cut bacon, scrambled eggs with shallots and goat cheese, sausage, smoked salmon and hash browns—all served family-style, so help yourself," he said as he poured her a cup of hot tea and handed it to her.

She took the teacup and set it down before serving herself, settling back on the settee and moaning as she took the first sip of her morning brew. "Heaven."

Spense smiled. "What's on your agenda for the day?"

"Anne, Sage, Rachel and I are meeting up in Sage's room for lunch and to get ready for the wedding."

"What does that entail? For men, it's usually booze and cigars, but it doesn't take all afternoon."

"That's because you don't have hair, makeup and intricate dresses to get into. But first we're going to have something to eat, and bitch about the men in our lives."

He cocked his head, eyes narrowed. "Last time I checked, you didn't have a man in your life."

"Do you check often?" she teased.

"As a matter of fact, I do."

She stopped her fork midway to her mouth. "Why?"

"Because if I'm to face serious opposition, I prefer to be prepared."

Saoirse wasn't sure how to respond to that. Ever since the night Anne, Sage and Rachel had slipped out of the Savoy to retrieve Anne's jewels from Wolsey's wine cellar, Spence hadn't made it easy for her to ignore him or the growing attraction she felt. She'd always found his physical good looks hard to resist, but more and more she recognized a great well of sensuality that called to a place deep within her she'd long thought dead.

He didn't press, his manners were impeccable, and he always treated her kindly. But it was as if he knew her dilemma where he was concerned—wildly attracted to a man with whom it would never work—and couldn't help saying provocative things to her. Ever since that night, he'd been disarmingly frank with her. He made sure she knew it was up to her, but that if and when she ever gave him the go-ahead, he was ready to step up in a major way.

"Okay, I'm going to ignore that for the time being.

The last time I was here, Corinne—that's the name of the night concierge, isn't it?" Spense nodded. "She mentioned that the Savoy has ghosts, and wondered if I'd ever seen any of them."

"And have you?"

"Yes, only one, and I've seen her since I was a child."

"I thought your first stay with us was when you came to help Rachel."

Saoirse nodded. "It was. The child visited me in Ireland for years. Then I didn't see her for a very long time. The first time I came here to help Rachel, I saw her on the elevator. And then this morning, I saw her in my room."

"The little girl in the yellow Victorian dress?"

"Yes. Have you seen her?"

"Not here in the hotel, but I saw her before I came through the Veil. I wasn't wholly sentient. I often wondered if she was one of our ghosts. Guests swear they've seen her getting on or off the elevator on the fifth floor. And others have seen her walking the stairs. Does she frighten you?"

"No. Until this morning, she'd never spoken. And this time, she sort of sang a little song." Saoirse looked at the notepad and repeated what the child had said:

"They did not search for those who died;
The chapel bell did not knell;
When the Irish witch can answer why,

> *Then our spirits will arise from Hell*
> *And with the King of Kings we will abide.*

"I'm assuming I'm the Irish witch in question," she concluded.

"I would think that was a fairly good assumption. No one has ever heard her speak that I know of. I take it you have no idea what she's talking about?"

"None. Does anyone have any idea who she is?"

"Not that I'm aware of. I'll tell you what—after the wedding, why don't you and I see what we can find?"

Saoirse waved off the idea, reluctant to accept the offer. "I don't want to take up your time. I know you're busy."

"I'm not so busy that I can't ensure your safety," he insisted. "I realize you're a witch, but dealing with the paranormal or supernatural is not a thing to be undertaken without a great deal of care, so you are not to pursue this unless you include me in whatever you're doing."

"Last time I checked, Spense, you didn't get a vote in what I do," she said, drawing herself up.

"That regal look works better for Anne. After all, she was a queen. And I refuse to stand on the sidelines and watch you get hurt."

"I thought it was my choice…"

"Whether or not we become romantically involved and you agree to submit to my authority?

Absolutely. But taking on some ghostly spirit all alone? Absolutely not."

"You don't get to make decisions about what I can and cannot do," she said, stomping her foot, which only provoked a smile from Spense.

"I think you will find in this hotel, I can influence a great deal of what happens to you."

"Hot news flash… the Savoy is *not* the only hotel in London."

"That is true, but it is the *best* hotel in London and the only one where two of your closest friends live and where another two work. Besides, the ghost is attached to this hotel."

"She came to me in Ireland, long before I heard about the Savoy. What makes you think she won't just follow me?"

"Because she never spoke to you before now, and because she has been attached to this hotel for more than a hundred years. Did it ever occur to you that she has allowed you to grow comfortable with her in your own home? You do know most people are not happy to be conversing with a ghost, don't you? Perhaps now that you're of a certain age and have obtained a certain level of power, the ghost believes you can help her find a place for her spirit to be at peace."

Saoirse crossed her arms, then realized the message her body language conveyed and quickly uncrossed them. "Shit. I hate it when you get all logical," she said with a pout.

"Watch your language, Saoirse. There is no need for you to curse—unless, I suppose, you are actually cursing someone. And I find that logic is most often helpful when trying to puzzle out something with which I am not familiar."

Saoirse switched tactics. "Do you know anything about her? I've tried researching her online, but I can only find the barest facts—little girl, yellow Victorian dress, attached to the Savoy. Nothing else."

"I've always been fascinated with her. So many people have seen her. I looked through the records kept during Queen Victoria's reign after the hotel was built—no incident reports or newspaper pieces. Either no one knew…"

"Or someone managed to kill the story."

Spense nodded. "I fear you are right."

"But that was more than a century ago. What possible harm could there come from my…"

"Our," he corrected.

Saoirse rolled her eyes. "From our investigating what happened to her?"

"This is England. Old jealousies, feuds and scandals run deep. Who knows who could still be interested in no one finding out? I suggest we talk to Rachel…"

"Spense." She liked the way he smiled when she

said his name. "Rachel is getting married this evening."

"I am aware. I am also aware that if she knew the little girl had contacted you, she would want to help. If we could sketch a picture of her dress, Rachel might be able to narrow it down to something more precise than simply 'the Victorian era.' That would at least give us a place to start. Then she and Holmes could go off on their honeymoon."

"Do you know where they're going?"

"I do. But you girls aren't the only ones good at keeping secrets."

CHAPTER 4

By the end of the evening, Rachel had wed Holmes and Anne had married Watson. The reception began and Spense was able to speak with several members of the Savoy's staff who had seen the little girl whom Saoirse had christened Victoria. Mazie, who worked for Gabe Watson in security, was also a talented artist and she'd managed to put together a sketch that was a good approximation of how the ghost looked, according to everyone Spense talked to. Once the cocktail party was well under way, Spense took the drawing out of his pocket and showed it to Saoirse.

"God, Spense, that looks just like her. It's remarkable. It's almost as if Mazie took a picture of her."

Watson leaned over and took the sketch. "That's our ghost, isn't it? The Yard screwed up big time when they didn't take Mazie on. Not only is she intelligent and a great shot, but she's also one hell of a sketch artist."

"What ghost?" asked Anne, who had been mingling with guests.

"The room is gorgeous," said Saoirse.

Anne smiled. "It's such a beautiful room. The murals and details of the walls meant we could keep the decorations simple."

"Simple, but stunning. I love the way you let the white flowers trail down the sides of the tall vases."

Anne reached out and took the sketch. "What a pretty little girl. She looks lost as if she was the one who was haunted, not the one doing the haunting."

Gabe's hand stroked down her back. "From the reign of Queen Victoria. People have been spotting her for as long as the Savoy has been around. She's never harmed anyone," Gabe assured her.

"Do you think the Warder of the Veil could help her cross over to the Light if we could somehow get her to him?" asked Saoirse.

Anne laughed ruefully. "I'm not sure, but I don't think we're on the Warder's holiday card list this year. Besides, unless she died at the Tower, I don't know that he could help her."

"What are we looking at?" asked Rachel as she came to stand behind Anne's shoulder. She took the sketch in her hand. "Who is she?"

"We don't know. She's a ghost here at the Savoy. A lot of people have seen her, but Spense said…"

"Spense?" asked Anne.

"That's what Saoirse calls me," answered Spense.

"Ah, like a pet name for a lover."

"Nothing like that," said Saoirse, entirely too quickly. "I just don't think Felix suits him."

"I agree," said Sage. "But in my defense, he didn't look like that—all lean predator—when I wrote and named him. I described him as round, kind of like Agatha Christie's *Poirot*. In fact, I based his physical description on Christie's famous Belgian detective. Trust me, Spense, if I'd known what you looked like, I might have still named you Felix Spenser, but everyone would have called you Spense."

Sage pointed at the sketch. "You know, I tried to do some research on her when I first got to the Savoy. The dearth of any details other than she exists, has a yellow dress, appears to be from the time of Victoria and likes the fifth floor here at the hotel kind of surprised me."

"It did me too," said Spense. "I looked through old records and newspaper clippings from that time but could find nothing. We were hoping Rachel could narrow down the year that dress might have been fashionable."

"Costumes and clothing are not my specialty, but I can see if anyone at Oxford might be able to help. I wouldn't set my hopes on that. The problem is, if she was a guest and was wealthy, it might tell us something. But she could just as easily have been a servant or an orphan and wearing hand-me-downs."

"Rachel," chided Holmes, "you can give them the names of your contacts, but we are leaving tonight at midnight."

"But if the ghost…"

"Has waited this long, she can wait a while longer. Give them the names. At least they'd have a place to start."

"Sometimes, Holmes, you're such a killjoy," said Rachel with a smile that implied she didn't believe that even for a minute.

"You should scan the picture and send it to Eddy. See if he can find out anything," suggested Roark.

"Already done," said Spense. "I like Rachel's idea about asking some folks who are experts in costumes. Did you know the Savoy was built by the producer of the Gilbert & Sullivan operettas? The site has been a palace, a hospital and then a theatre. They cleared away the remnants. In fact, the hotel was built on top of the ruins of the hospital next to the Savoy Theatre that he had built especially for the operettas, and which still exists."

Watson laughed. "Don't get him started. As well as being the head concierge, Spense could easily be the hotel's historian. He's forgotten more about the hotel's history than the rest of us will ever care to know."

"So there was a hospital here before the hotel?"

asked Saoirse. Spense nodded. "That could be the reason she talked about there being more than just her."

"Talked?" said Rachel.

"Yes. I've seen her for years. This morning she talked to me. Well, she kind of sang a little rhyme to me. It wasn't all that good, but I definitely got the impression that her spirit as well as that of several others were trapped here, and they think I can help them."

"People in my time had a much more substantial belief in ghosts and spirits than we do now," said Anne. "It was said if one talked to you, you needed to do as they asked or get a priest to exorcise their spirit, which was just another money-making scheme by the Pope and his Church. Are we going to help?"

"We," said Watson, "are going to Paris."

"We're going to Paris?" asked Rachel excitedly, looking at Holmes.

"Oh, hell no," he groaned. "I'm not taking you anywhere that had anything to do with the Wars of the Roses or the Tudor dynasty. We're getting on a cruise ship, where I can keep you locked up and naked in our cabin."

"That sounds so much better than Paris," said Anne.

"Don't worry, sweetheart," said Watson. "I made sure our hotel had a big balcony from which you can see the Eiffel Tower, while no one can see us. It also has sound-proof walls and kick-ass room service. What makes you think once I get you inside, I won't strip you naked and have at you for the next ten days?"

Anne grinned lasciviously. "Promise?"

Watson laughed as he leaned over to kiss her. "Absolutely."

The wedding reception proceeded with everyone laughing and celebrating. Just before they took their leave, Anne pulled Spense aside. "You will watch over her, won't you? I can't stand the thought of something happening to one of you."

Spense lifted her hand to his lips. "I give you my word, Milady. She is safe in my care."

"Oh, I'm not sure I like that," said Anne as Watson joined her.

"Is she now? It's about damn time," Watson said. "Come on, babe, I've got a limo waiting and we're going to cross the Channel tonight. We should be in Paris tomorrow morning."

Anne's eyebrow quirked up. "Don't we have to wait for the tide?"

"Nope. We will be on a boat with a motor…"

"Like in the car?"

Watson nodded. "More like the train, but yes."

"Can we fool around in the back of the limo like we did in the train car?"

"Yes, baby. I promise, we can fuck as often as you like."

"In that case, what are we waiting for?" she asked with a smile.

"She's going to be the death of you," Spense told Watson.

The other man shrugged. "Maybe, but what a way to go."

He and Anne grasped hands and ran to meet their driver. Meanwhile, it appeared that Rachel was more interested in helping with the ghost than going on her honeymoon. Spense could see them arguing and understood why Holmes had wanted Rachel away from anything that dealt with history. He watched as Holmes reached the end of his patience, tossed Rachel over his shoulder and left the room to much laughter and catcalling.

"Kind of high-handed," said Saoirse, sitting down next to him and nodding to Sage, who waved, as she left with Roark.

Spense handed her a piece of the wedding cake she had been trying to avoid. "Are you sure you won't have a piece of the cake? It's delicious. As for being a bit high-handed, I don't necessarily disagree. But sometimes a Dom needs to exert his authority in order to get his beloved sub the peace and relaxation she needs."

"I will have to admit, I've never seen Rachel happier, and I think he's at the center of that."

"I would say the same of Holmes. Helping her achieve her dreams, making sure she gets all that she needs and desires, that's at the heart of how a Dom serves his sub."

Saoirse looked up at him, skeptically. "So, it isn't just the sub serving the Dom?"

This was a different and interesting take on the whole Dom/sub lifestyle her friends had all embraced. She'd never thought of Rachel as submissive and had been surprised she'd acquiesced as quickly and easily as she had to Holmes' brand of dominance. She was coming to realize it wasn't a question of one size fits all but that each relationship defined its own boundaries and parameters.

"Not in my opinion. Oh, we Doms may call it worshiping our subs, but it's the same thing. I find great satisfaction in helping the subs I train find themselves and figure out what they need."

"Don't they all fall in love with you?"

"No. Part of my job as a training Dom is to ensure that doesn't happen. If and when I finally collar a sub of my own, I will step down as a training Dom. I don't think I could act as a disciplinarian for anyone after that."

"So do Holmes or Watson do any training?" she asked curiously.

"Holmes used to, but not any more for the same reason. Watson was always a very popular Dom, but he never gave any sub a reason to believe he wanted something more than what he offered in the club.

Apparently, one of the subs thought she'd challenge Anne…"

Saoirse laughed. "Now that, I would have liked to see. My guess is the other sub fared too well."

"Interestingly, Milady didn't so much as lay a finger on her, but her ability to dress someone down with regal authority is second to none. So much so that Jordan James—she and Fitzwallace, her husband/Dom own the club—have become fast friends. Neither Watson nor Fitzwallace were amused."

"Sometimes I think about what Anne has gone through. I think she's made a remarkable adjustment."

Spense nodded. "As do I, but a lot of that is because she wanted to. The other night, I remarked that I hadn't heard as many snarky comments from her about Henry of late."

"She has a right to hate him."

"I couldn't agree more," Spense explained. "It was a casual observation, and I ensured she knew that. And then she told me the most extraordinary thing. She said she decided her heart had only so much capacity for feeling. She said she figured out she could continue to hate Henry and love Gabe a little less or let her hatred for Henry burn to ash and blow away with the wind and love Gabe a little more. She chose to love Gabe with all of her heart."

"I admire her. She always had such courage and

intelligence. Unfortunately, her first husband didn't value either. I think a lot of us have lousy ex-husbands. I suppose I should be grateful mine didn't chop off my head—although had it been an option for him, he might have welcomed it."

"Then it's a good thing he's your ex-husband. Both he and Henry were fools," Spense said firmly. "I've never thought of Elizabeth I as Henry's daughter; I've always thought of her as Anne's."

"The four of us went to Elizabeth's grave, and she wept. Even though she saw most of the major events in her daughter's life, she wasn't there for her. Do you know if Bloody Mary had killed Elizabeth when she threw her in the Tower, Anne had decided to go with her into the Light?"

"Thank God she didn't—for a myriad of reasons, but mostly because Anne is the light of Watson's life."

"Watson strikes me as a guy who's lived a pretty happy life."

"Not always," said Spense. "He, like everyone else, has his demons. He's just brave enough and honorable enough to keep them at bay and bask in the light that Anne has brought him. I know the four of you think the four of us are too protective, and I'm not sure I'm convinced you actually need us. I like to think, though, that we do make things a bit easier for you."

"A bit," Saoirse agreed, laughing.

The delightful sound of her amusement took a

weight off Spense's shoulders. What he wouldn't give to hear her laugh more, all because he knew exactly how to make her smile.

"I have the day off tomorrow," he ventured. "Why don't you call up those two people at Oxford, and I'll call the head of costuming over at the Savoy Theatre? We'll see if we can't help this little girl."

"So, you're really in? You'll really help me?" Her eyes were wide with hope, a look that endeared her to him even more.

Spense grinned at her. "As Holmes always says to Watson, *the game's afoot.*"

"What does that even mean?" she asked.

He shrugged. "I have absolutely no idea, but it always sounds so positive and like something exciting is about to happen… And it usually does."

CHAPTER 5

Spense accompanied Saoirse to her room and, as with Anne, gallantly kissed her hand. Then he opened her door and waited to leave until she had closed and locked it.

He was a curious man. She had felt the sexual attraction between them all evening, but he'd never pushed, not once. He'd been attentive and had seen to her every need, in sharp contrast to her ex-husband. She wanted to talk to someone, but it had been obvious that Roark had plans for Sage or vice versa. Either way, neither would appreciate a late-night phone call. Rachel and Anne were off with their new husbands on their honeymoons.

Oh! She knew just who to talk with. Corinne—the hotel's night concierge—was probably around, and she might know something. After all, she'd been the first Savoy staff person to talk to her about the ghost.

Saoirse called down to the front desk and confirmed that Corinne was working that night. Then, headed down to the lobby in search of her.

The minute she got on the elevator, she could feel the drop in temperature.

"Victoria? Are you here?" she asked softly.

The little girl in the yellow dress appeared, her expression worried. "I shouldn't have said anything. They don't want anyone to know."

"I have friends who want to help. We want to help you and the others to the light."

"Be careful," the ghost warned. "They murdered us and have killed all those who thought to solve the riddle."

"Am I the Irish witch who is supposed to answer why or was there another Irish witch?"

Victoria nodded. "There was, but she was killed by a monster. She knew about us and wanted others to know, but he killed her before she could tell anyone. Be careful, Saoirse. I wouldn't want to see you killed."

The little girl turned and walked back through the elevator doors right before the lift came to a stop at the lobby. *So, the little girl knows my name. Anne was right; those caught between the land of the living and the great beyond were aware of what transpired.* The doors opened, and Saoirse found herself staring at Corinne.

"The front desk said you were looking for me. Are you feeling all right? You look like you've seen a ghost," said the night concierge.

"Funny you should say that. I just saw Victoria—that's what I call the ghost of the little girl in the Victorian dress."

"I saw the sketch Mazie did. It was eerie."

"Is Spense still here?"

"Who?"

"Spense. Sorry. Felix. That just seems like a terrible name for him, so I've taken to calling him Spense."

"I like that," Corinne said, her face brightening. "I think he's still here. Come on, let's see if we can't find him." Corinne took her past the front desk, and down the hall to the private offices.

"I knew Gabe had an office; I didn't know Spense did," said Saoirse.

"He's the first concierge ever given one. I think management is afraid he'll leave. I swear if he left, half the guests would want to know where he'd gone so they could change accommodations. He makes what he does look so easy. I only hope that someday I'll be even half as good."

"I know for a fact he depends on you. He told me once he no longer worries about the hotel when you're on duty."

"Wow. That's high praise coming from Fe… Spense." Corinne grinned. "I'm going to spread the word."

Saoirse returned her smile as Corinne knocked on

the door. "Spense? It's Corinne. I have Saoirse with me."

The door opened, and Spense showed them in. Spense's office seemed to reflect both the elegance of the rest of the hotel and his own personal taste. The furnishings were timeless—filled with antiques and she thought carefully chosen and curated details. She smiled seeing what she assumed was one of the paintings Monet did while staying at the Savoy.

Saoirse paused, taking in what she was seeing. The concierge clearly had been in the midst of changing clothes. His shoes were off, his shirt and tuxedo jacket laying neatly across the back of a chair. He still had on a white tank t-shirt with his black tuxedo pants, and he'd pulled his suspenders back up. While he always looked good, the t-shirt showed off his muscular torso and arms. He wasn't bulky muscle like Holmes or Watson, but sleeker—more like a predatory jaguar than a bear.

The man was incredibly handsome in a suit, gorgeous in a tuxedo, but like this? Drool-worthy. What would it be like to touch that gorgeous physique? She gave a soft, longing sigh.

"Is everything all right? You aren't sick, Saoirse, are you?" Spense asked solicitously.

She breathed in deeply, hoping she hadn't blushed. "No. I'm fine. I was headed down to pick Corinne's brain about the ghost. She rode down the elevator with me…"

"The ghost, not me," supplied Corinne.

"But she talked to me," said Saoirse. "And she knew my name."

"Did she repeat the riddle?" asked Spense.

"No. She said they'd been murdered, and the killer had kept it quiet. She talked about the Irish witch trying to stop him."

"But you weren't alive at the time of Queen Victoria," said Corinne.

"No," Saoirse said, looking at Spense. "But there was another Irish witch who was."

The color drained from Spense's face, and he stumbled back. Saoirse and Corinne both reached out to steady him. Saoirse was surprised at how much she didn't like Corinne hanging onto his arm.

"Are you all right, sir?" asked Corinne.

Spense seemed to recover quickly. "I'm fine, Corinne. Why don't you get back to your duties? I'll take care of Ms. Madigan."

Corinne shot him a wicked grin. "You do know you're the only one on staff who calls her that, right? The rest of us call her Saoirse, and some of us call her miracle worker. She has the most amazing muscle-relaxing salve."

"Did it help your hamstring?" Saoirse asked.

"Yep. I gave some to Burt for his back. He said he needs to see you before you leave."

"Can you see how many people want some? I can

head over to Rachel's place and make a big batch for the staff to share."

"Dispensing medicine without a license is a crime," said Spense, his voice stern.

She couldn't tell if he was serious or just giving her a hard time. It was often difficult to tell with Spense. "It's just herbs and plant extracts. Nothing illegal, I promise, although I do have a compounding license for Ireland and the entire UK. You can come watch if you like."

"No, I believe you."

"Well, I'll leave you two alone," said Corinne cheekily before leaving.

Saoirse was determined not to think about Spense's gorgeous body. Instead, she focused on how her Gift could give some poor souls peace. "Irish witch? Victorian England? Sound like anyone we know?" she asked.

Spense nodded. "Mary Jane Kelly." He winced, as though someone had punched him in the gut.

Mary Jane Kelly had been Jack the Ripper's last victim and had cursed him into a mirror. The Ripper had escaped and attached itself to Rachel, who had gone to Scotland Yard—where she'd met Holmes. The group had worked together and been able to send the Ripper to Hell once and for all. But it had been no easy task. He didn't like the coincidence of that evil killer's name popping up again now, when Saoirse could be in danger.

"You don't think the Ripper killed them, do you?" he asked.

"I have no idea. Maybe he did; or maybe Mary Jane Kelly got too close to finding the killer, and someone set the Ripper on her. We do know that whoever she sent into the mirror killed her and that we sent him to Hell."

"You don't think he's gotten out, do you?"

Saoirse laughed. "It's easy to see you're not Irish. Trust me, when the banshees drag you to Hell, you're not going anywhere. Those ladies don't mess around."

Spense leaned against his desk, tapping his thighs as he pondered the situation. "If the Ripper didn't kill the ghost, but was sent to kill Mary Jane Kelly—did the same man murder the other four victims who were attributed to the Ripper?"

"I thought those five were confirmed to have been killed by the Ripper, with an additional six with varying degrees of similarity sometimes being attributed to him as well."

"Yes, but who knows what's true? Could some of the killings have been the work of copycats?"

"Could be," Saoirse said, nodding. "In fact, there are several conspiracy theories about the Ripper. Some say there was a group or cult who did the killing, while others think Queen Victoria's grandson, Prince Albert Victor, committed some—and the Crown covered it up and obscured the facts by staging similar killings at times where he had an iron-tight alibi."

"Not beyond the realm of possibility. But there's not much we can do about it tonight. I can send Eddy a message and ask him to expand his search regarding the ghost and have him look into Prince Albert Victor."

"Ask him to include Dr. William Gull in his searches around the prince."

"Who is Gull?" asked Spense.

"He was a physician who cured Prince Albert Victor supposedly of typhoid, but the prince is also believed to have had syphilis," Saoirse explained. "There are all kinds of theories and speculation about what happened, why it happened, and no real way to separate facts from rumors. In fact, some of those who think he could have been the Ripper think it was because the syphilis had driven him mad and that when the disease had ravaged him, Gull may have helped him to die—either at Queen Victoria's request or with her permission."

"That's a blood-chilling thought even a century later."

His words made her wonder about his experience coming from a book into the real world. "Is the passage of time ever odd to you?" she asked. "I mean, I learned about Queen Victoria and Jack the Ripper in school. For you, everything is just like yesterday."

"Sage wrote us with full backstories and when we

emerged, we did so as if we'd always been here. I find myself talking to staff about things that happened years ago—when I was still trapped in the books—and yet, I remember it as if I were there."

"Is that how it felt—like you were trapped?"

He shook his head. "Another curiosity. While I was in the book, I wasn't really aware of feeling confined, though I did feel discontented somehow. When I first came out into the real world, I loved the freedom but worried I'd be sucked back into the book. Gradually, that concern faded as we seemed to be here to stay. It's only recently that I realized the book had, in a way, trapped me. Please don't say anything to Sage. It would upset her to know we weren't happy. Let me get a shirt on, and I'll take you back to your room."

"I can get back to my room on my own, but I don't think I can sleep."

"Would you like a nightcap?" he asked.

What was the saying? Go big or go home! At first, she'd fought her growing attraction to Spense—they were so different. But the longer she was around him, the less the differences seemed to matter.

"Would you like to have it in my room? Maybe have something brought up?"

"I'm not sure that's a good idea, Saoirse…"

So much for that idea.

"Okay. I'll be fine getting upstairs by myself. The

Savoy is good at keeping the riffraff out, present company excluded," she said, turning to leave.

Spense reached out and took hold of her arm to stop her as he closed the distance between them. "You need to let me finish. I worry that it's not a good idea because I wouldn't want to leave—not until morning at least."

She faced him, not knowing how to respond. Spense took that option away from her as he leaned down and pressed his lips to hers. Arousal surged through her system—her nipples peaked, and her pussy began to soften and get wet.

For heaven's sake, it's just a kiss and a very polite one at that.

His lips moved against hers, not overpoweringly, but enticing, seducing—teasing at hers to judge her response and coax her to engage. When she didn't pull away, Spense's hand left her arm so that he could circle her waist and pull her closer. It wasn't as if she hadn't noticed that he appeared to be well-endowed, but now with his manhood pulsing against her belly, his desire was hard to ignore. A shudder went through her body... It had been so long since she'd been with someone.

When his tongue ran along the seam of her lips, Saoirse parted them, letting him in. Before she could think about how a man whose lips felt so gentle on hers could be considered a Dom, he deepened the kiss. In the next instant, it transformed from question to demand as his tongue slid into her mouth, taking command—dancing and tangling with hers.

Spense's fingers twisted in her hair as his other arm tightened around her, taking even greater control of the encounter. She could understand why he was so popular at the club—every inch a gentleman until someone took the leash off. And then the domesticated house cat metamorphosed into a very large, very predatory jungle cat. It was intoxicating.

Now she understood why he had warned her. It wasn't that he didn't want her; he hadn't known she wanted him. She would clear that up for him. Saoirse wound her arms around his neck, nestling closer to his warmth and feeling safer than she ever had before.

He lifted his head. "Say yes, Saoirse. Give over to me. I'll take care of you."

"Aren't you afraid it will be difficult to go back to being just friends?"

"I hate that term, *just friends*. There's nothing wrong with being friends, but why would we go back? I've wanted you from the first time you entered the Savoy. I think you're the most enchanting, gorgeous, sensual creature who ever existed."

In another time, in another place and with someone else, she might have questioned that, but the man standing in front of her looking down at her was not a man given to deception. Somehow, he knew just what to say to make her believe.

"Say yes," he repeated, pressing into her, allowing

her to feel the length and rigidity of his need as his hand slipped from her waist and down to cup her ass, holding her in place.

Saoirse nodded, unable to form coherent words.

"Say it," he commanded, and she understood why they called it dominance.

"Yes," she managed to whisper before his mouth closed on hers. He turned her around, backing her up to his desk and lifting her so that she was sitting on the edge, with him standing between her legs.

He gently drew the hem of her dress up past her knees until it was pooled at the juncture of her torso and legs. His hand slipped between her thighs, and had he not been kissing her deeply, she would have screamed with pleasure as he brushed his hand over her clit. His finger traced down from her swollen nub to her labia, parting her wet folds.

"Hmm... I think my wicked little witch may be a bit of a wanton as well," he murmured.

"I'm..."

Before she could apologize for getting his hand wet, although he was the one who put it there, he nipped her ear.

"Don't you dare apologize to me when I'm the one who should be apologizing. I should have let you know how I felt long before now. I won't make that kind of mistake with you in the future."

"Do you see us as having a future beyond tonight?"

Spence growled and brought his hand up to tweak her nipple. Even though she had on a bra and dress, neither was made of overly thick material—and it hurt. Interestingly, while she could feel the discomfort in her pebbled peak, she could also feel a corresponding pleasure shoot straight into her pussy. She was beginning to understand what her friends saw in the whole D/s lifestyle.

Saoirse had never felt anything when her ex had tried to get them involved with BDSM. She'd felt uncomfortable mentally, unsafe physically and ignored emotionally. She was beginning to believe she would feel none of those things with Spense. Oh, he might nip her ear or pinch her nipple, but she responded to him in a whole different way than she had with her ex. Both his behavior and her sense of safety with him helped her to focus entirely on him.

"Yes. I think we might just have the most spectacular future together," he insisted. "I know that's what I want, but if you don't, we need to end this before we get started. Tell me you can feel it too."

She nodded. "I can, but it scares the hell out of me."

"That's all right, sweetheart, you'll see I'm right. Anything that scares you will have to go through me to get to you."

Then there was no more time for talking as his mouth captured hers and his hand skimmed back down to tease and pleasure her pussy. Every time her body raced toward the edge of climax, he pulled his hand away, but only until he sensed the orgasm was retreating, and then he'd begin again. Over and over, he teased and played until she thought she would scream.

"Tsk, tsk," he whispered against her lips. "You're going to learn that submission starts with patience… and trust."

Spense left his thumb on her throbbing clit as he penetrated and stroked her pussy. Saoirse couldn't remember the last time she'd felt this alive, this sexual, this good. She sighed with contentment and need into his mouth.

He chuckled—a wicked, seductive sound. "Do you want to come here on my desk before I take you upstairs and ravish you?"

"Yes," she managed to moan.

"Yes, sir," he corrected.

"Yes, sir. Please, sir."

"Good girl," he crooned as a second finger joined the first up inside her. He curled them both upward, stretching and filling her, working his own kind of magick.

He thrust his fingers in and out of her—sometimes deep, sometimes shallow—his thumb hovering over her clit, but never quite touching. Saoirse arched her back, wanting his fingers to plunge in deep and hard. Spense pulled his hand back.

"Did that work with your ex?"

She couldn't contain the bitter laugh. "He didn't care as long as he got to stick his dick in me somewhere."

"Regardless of what he may have called himself, if he wasn't ensuring your pleasure and happiness, he was no Dom."

Smiling, she said, "Please, sir."

CHAPTER 6

Saoirse had a lot to learn. Her ex-husband had taught her a lot of bad habits, but Spense wasn't known as the most patient of the training Doms at Baker Street for nothing. He found it interesting that she had taken to calling him Spense. She wasn't the only one who didn't care for the moniker Sage had labeled him with. At the club, he was known as Master Spenser.

He went back to kissing her. He thought there was a very real possibility that he could get lost in kissing Saoirse, especially if he could play with her pussy at the same time. She was so responsive. It was clear to him that she had convinced herself she wasn't submissive because the one time she had admitted it, she'd been burned. But they could work through that.

Again and again, he stroked her pussy. Saoirse learned quickly. Relaxed, she lay back, propped up on her elbows, letting him lead. Curling his fingers up, he slid them along her G-spot as he allowed himself the luxury of plundering her mouth. Faster and faster he caressed her sex, until her hips were moving, not because she was trying to get her own way but because she had given over and was enjoying her pleasure. As she rode the crest of the wave, Spense pressed his thumb against her clit hard, and she fell over the edge.

He loved watching a sub climax from his attention and skill, but this was different. This was Saoirse, and this moment felt better to him than anything he'd done before. He could see the orgasm coursing through her system, making her skin flush and her pussy cream against his hand. He didn't move, just let her come back to herself. When the shaking had stopped, he removed his fingers and brought them up to his mouth, sucking them clean as she watched, her eyes riveted on his hand.

"God, you taste sweet, like wild honey mixed with cream."

He stepped back, drew the hem of her dress back down and slipped on his shirt, before extending his hand to her. Tentatively, she took it.

"Do you want me to…" she started.

"What I want is for you to do precisely as you just did. Let me show you how good things are going to be between us."

"But I don't think it's fair…"

"Fair is what I say it is. I will solicit your input and you can, of course, always say no. Did you have a safeword before?"

Again, the bitter laugh. Spense might need to locate her ex and punch him in the nose.

"The kind of relationship Sage, Rachel and Anne all have is completely foreign to me. With the exception of my ex, I've always had to be the one in charge. The one time I wasn't, it wasn't pretty and left a bad taste in my mouth."

"I'll have to see if I can remedy that."

She cocked her head to one side, her eyes softening. "I am actually beginning to believe you might be able to do that."

Spense grinned. "I'll make a believer of you. I'd like to take you upstairs to your room."

"Not afraid of that walk of shame?" she teased.

He stopped and turned her to look at him full on. "Nothing—I repeat, nothing I do with you would ever be shameful to me. I am proud to walk at your side and have people know we are together. I would also never want to embarrass you. I'll ensure that no one sees me in the morning, and I keep an extra change of clothes here in my office. I can be the soul of discretion until you feel comfortable allowing our friends and others to know we are together. Understood?"

She nodded. "You really are almost too good to be true. I know Rachel and Holmes had a contract in place, but then again, I don't think Anne and Gabe ever did."

"Nor did Sage and Roark, but if you would feel more comfortable having one, that isn't a problem."

"Let me get this straight—you give me a mind-blowing orgasm and are willing to wait for a contract to be drawn up?"

"Yes. D/s won't work without open, honest communication. If you're uncomfortable, it's my responsibility to do whatever is necessary to alleviate your concerns."

"I thought Doms liked to push their sub's boundaries…"

"We do. But that doesn't mean you back someone into a corner and ignore their concerns—at least, that's not something I would do. Pushing boundaries comes from having earned your partner's trust so they are willing to try."

"I suppose it's easier for me because I do know you and trust you. I don't need a contract and for the record, I'm on birth control and I'm clean."

"So am I—well, the clean part anyway. By the way, I like the fact that you weren't wearing panties."

"Good. Because I absolutely loathe them. Every once in a while, I'll get talked into buying them when I'm shopping with the girls and then I don't wear them."

He stood by her side, opened the door and walked her to the elevator. When the doors opened, he led her inside the car and pressed the button for the fifth floor.

"I'll see you upstairs," he said quietly and then withdrew, giving several other people the opportunity to step on before the doors slid closed.

As soon as Saoirse disappeared, Spense walked through the lobby, waving to the night people at the front desk and headed outside. As he headed down the sidewalk, he let the cool, breezy air soothe his heated skin. He turned the corner so he could access the freight entrance and take one of the service elevators to her floor, giving both of them time for a breather.

Riding up the elevator, he forced his head to be clear. Not unzipping his fly to shove his hard cock up inside her before she had a chance to fully recover from her orgasm had been one of the most difficult things he'd ever done. Saoirse needed to learn from the get-go that her pleasure and satisfaction were important to him, and he would almost always see to her needs first.

As he neared the fifth floor, the temperature in the lift went from warm to chilly in an instant and the ghost of Victoria appeared before him. He'd never seen her before here in the real world. He'd caught only glimpses of her when he had existed in the pages of Sage's books, and he'd met several of the other resident ghosts in both book and this world, but never her—until now. She stared at him with her sad, haunted eyes, but said nothing, proceeding to exit the elevator on the fifth floor before the doors opened. When they did open and he stepped into the hallway, no one was there.

Spense went to Saoirse's room and knocked softly. She opened the door dressed only in a beautiful silk and lace robe. She stepped back and allowed him to enter. He closed the door and turned to secure the night latch. When he turned back around, Saoirse had untied the sash that held the dressing gown closed and let it fall open to reveal her lush body.

God, his imagination had not done her justice—beautiful breasts that would overflow his hands, dusky areolas with darker pebbled nipples in their center; a delicate, nipped-in waist; and hips that begged to be held onto when a man took her from behind.

She bit her lip, looking apprehensive. "I wasn't sure what you wanted…"

"You, Saoirse. I only want you."

Spense stepped forward and slid the robe from her shoulders before he swept her off her feet and carried her into the bedroom. She had only reserved a room, not the suite she had now, but both Holmes and Watson had upgraded her—as if Spense wouldn't have done it himself. He'd have to make sure the front desk knew to charge her stay to his house account.

He laid her on the bed, setting her ass on the edge and then kneeling, placing each of her legs on either side of his head. Breathing in the scent of her renewed and previously satiated arousal, he licked his lips and heard her catch her breath. Leaning in, he stroked her with his tongue, licking her from the opening to her wet heat up to her clit. He circled that delicate nub, and then licked back down.

Spence looked up. "As you don't have a safeword…"

"I came up with one—Abracadabra. Trust me, it isn't a word I ever use, despite what all the books, movies and television series would have you think."

"Abracadabra. I like it." He chuckled, then grew serious again. "I'll try not to make you use it, but if you do, we'll take a break and talk about it. So, unless I hear it, I'm just going to assume you're comfortable with whatever I'm doing."

Lowering his head to her sex, he gently tasted every inch of her labia before spearing her with his tongue. Saoirse arched her back in response, not in demand, which pleased him, and he licked up all the cream that remained from her previous climax in his office. As he suckled her, he could feel her softening all over again—her pussy readying itself for his use…

And use it, he would. Come tomorrow morning, she would be sore from the number of times he'd fucked her throughout the night. He'd been waiting for some signal from her that she was interested, and he'd finally received it. Now, he wouldn't hold back on his desire for her.

Spense brought his mouth down and enveloped

her clit with it, latching on as he pushed a finger inside her pussy. He opened his eyes to see her watching him intently. He held her gaze as he suckled, strengthening their connection and aiming to prevent her from raising any walls between them.

Saoirse chewed on her lower lip, as if trying to hold back not just the physical feeling but the emotional bond that was building. He was determined to push through that fear and prove to her she could trust him. For now, he focused on pleasuring her, adoring her… until finally, she flung her head back and moaned as her hands reached for his head. She couldn't keep still as his tongue and finger worked in perfect rhythm to send her over the edge into another climax that engulfed her entire body. She tightened against his mouth and hands, coming for him, and then relaxed into the bed with a sigh.

Spense rolled back onto his feet and stood, lifting her into the center of the mattress and removing his clothes without ever breaking eye contact. When he was naked, she opened her arms and welcomed him into her bed.

His body had never felt so alive—not inside the books or since he'd escaped. He now understood in a way he hadn't allowed himself to what Roark, Holmes and even Watson had come to know and cherish. This woman was his, and he would do everything in his power to ensure she never wanted to be anything else. He took pleasure in noticing she was watching him with desire, her eyes widening and then smiling appreciatively at the sight of his fully erect cock. He sent a silent thanks to Sage that she had ensured all the men in her books were well hung.

Kneeling on the bed, he reached for her and lay down beside her, kissing her deeply and allowing her to taste herself on his tongue. As she moaned, Spense rolled on top of her, easily parting her thighs and making a place for himself. The heat of her pussy called to his cock in a way that he'd never known before. He lowered himself carefully, letting her bear all of his weight as his cock homed in on its target. He captured her mouth, plunging his tongue deep inside hers as he surged forward, entering, and filling her with one long, hard push.

Saoirse's legs entwined with his, and she arched her back as her arms came up to encircle him. She writhed beneath him as he began to stroke inside her, dragging himself back before plunging in again. Her pussy tightened, trying to keep his cock in place, and he smiled as he kissed her.

Spense reached under her and grasped the globes of her ass—holding and steadying her so he could plunder her pussy at will. God, she was tight and wet and fabulous. Nothing and no one had ever felt this good. The ache in his soul that he had known from his first moment of sentience was healed by the way she held him and kissed him with wild abandon.

This was no quiet little sub. Saoirse was an incredibly passionate woman. He doubted she'd settle in like Rachel or Sage. No, the dance for dominance would always be there, and he found himself looking forward to it.

He gripped her firmly as he began to pound into her. Her nails raked his back, and she cried his name as she came, her pussy clamping down on his length as he continued to thrust in and out of her. There would come a time he would have her on her knees in front of him, her upper torso lowered onto the mattress, but this first time he wanted the intimacy that only face-to-face could offer. He didn't just want to focus on how good her wet heat felt as it contracted around his dick; he wanted to be kissing her, feeling her nails scoring his flesh.

Her body responded so beautifully to his possession. He reveled in being with her, inside her, pleasuring her. Over and over he fucked in and then out, only to drive back into her. He wanted to learn every sigh, every moan, every scream. Her pussy seemed made for him, and her body fit his as though Sage had written her to be his perfect partner.

"Spense," she cried.

"I've got you, Saoirse. I've got you."

She was fierce and wanton, sweet and sensual. She was everything he'd ever wanted and all those things he hadn't known he needed.

Her body tightened around him again, and he let loose his own primal being, giving over to his own lust. He slammed into her again and again, all finesse forgotten as he gloried in being inside her and provoking her own primitive response. Saoirse's body bowed as she all but howled in pleasure, giving him license to ravage her pussy like a man long denied. He drove into her a final time, holding himself hard against her as he flooded her with his cum.

When the storm had passed, he lay atop her softness while she stroked his back and nuzzled his neck.

"That was... I don't even have words for what that was," she breathed.

Neither did he as he rolled off her body and pulled her close. "Perfection. Ecstasy. Absolute bliss."

"You'll stay with me? Be here when I wake up?" she said sleepily.

He chuckled and whispered, "I'll be the one waking you up throughout the night to have you again."

"Perfection," she agreed as she cuddled close to him, wrapping her arm across his chest and resting her head on his shoulder.

For the first time since he had escaped from Sage's written world, he knew what it was to fear somehow being returned, but knew that like Roark and Holmes, he would give his life before he would leave Saoirse.

CHAPTER 7

*S*pense had been as good as his word. He remained with her throughout the night and woke her several times to have his carnal way with her. She knew she would be stiff and sore when she tried to get up. She'd used muscles and moved in ways she hadn't in years. But she didn't care. The elated and exaggerated feeling of well-being that infused her body and soul were worth a few aches and pains.

He'd left while it was still dark, slipping quietly from her bed to dress. He kissed her and told her to let him know when she was awake, and he'd have breakfast sent up to her. She fussed and tried to drag him back to bed for one more round.

"No," she said, clutching his arm. "Come back to bed."

"Saoirse, sweetheart, I have to go to work. But call

me when you wake up and I'll have breakfast sent up to you."

"Later. Come back to bed. Just one more time, please?"

He chuckled. "No. That's enough for now. You're going to be sore as it is."

"But I'm so happy. I want more…"

Quicker than she thought was possible, he pulled her toward him and flipped her onto her belly, smacking her ass three times with a distinctive crack. Pain blossomed across her backside.

"Enough. If I didn't have to work, I'd like nothing more than to remain in bed with you. Last night surpassed not only every experience I've ever had, but every fantasy. You are the most beguiling creature on this earth, and I will never get enough of you. Now, go back to sleep and I'll see you later. Don't forget to call me when you wake up."

"That hurt, you know," she said, pouting.

"Not as much as it will if you don't settle down."

He stood up and looked down at her, one eyebrow quirked.

"Yes, sir. I'm sorry. I just never knew sex could be that amazing and wonderful."

He leaned down and brushed his lips against hers. "That's because it was more than just sex. That, my beautiful, wanton witch, was making love and it was extraordinary."

He kissed her a final time and then left quietly.

She had to admit she agreed with him. That had been so much more than sex. She rolled back on her back, winced and then smiled. There had been a bit of sting, but it had morphed into remembered pleasure, and her entire body had begun to sing the song he had taught her.

When she woke after a few hours of undisturbed sleep, she rolled over and dialed the head concierge's desk.

"Good morning, sweetheart," he said in a deep voice that sounded as rich as dark chocolate.

"You'd better be able to tell whose room it is that's calling you," she purred.

"I am indeed. Would you like me to have breakfast sent up to you? I can't get away at the moment."

"How much trouble would I be in if I made some completely inappropriate response to that?"

"Five more than you got this morning. But if you behave yourself, we can have lunch downstairs."

"Don't trust me, huh?" she teased, twirling her finger in her hair as she mercilessly flirted.

"No. I don't trust myself. You naked is far too tempting."

She grinned, delighted. "You say the sweetest things. What time works for you? I have things I want to do, but nothing at a specific time."

"Would one o'clock be too late?" he asked.

"No, we're good. You do know I don't normally sleep this late, don't you?"

"Yes, and I also know I didn't let you get much sleep. Your breakfast should be up to you in thirty minutes, and I'll see you at one."

"Thank you. And would you think I was too mushy if I told you last night was the best night of my life and that I'm going to miss you until I see you again?"

"Not at all. I would say ditto to the latter and that I'll have to try harder for the former."

"Trust me, sir, you were more than hard enough last night."

"Saoirse…"

"Sorry. I'll see you later."

"Behave yourself."

She smiled as she hung up the phone. *I'm going to have so much fun bedeviling him.* She swung her legs over the side of the bed, sat up and groaned. Not only was her bottom still tender, but all of her girly parts groaned in protest and then wanted to know where he was. Laughing, she hurried into the shower, made herself up, and pulled on leggings, a sports bra and an oversized, slouchy sweater. She set aside a pair of boots to pull on when she was ready to leave her room.

When room service knocked, she opened the door, allowing the wait staff inside to set up her breakfast on the table. It hadn't escaped her notice that her room had been upgraded from a simple room to a suite. She suspected Rachel or Anne had done it—

Anne was the more likely suspect as Gabe worked for the Savoy. She did notice that there was also a small bouquet of kaleidoscope roses in a small vase and rather imagined those were from Spense.

"So, what did he send me?" she asked.

"An omelet with ham, cheddar cheese, red and orange peppers and caramelized onions. There's also bacon, roasted red potato hash and an English muffin. And of course, orange juice and Irish breakfast tea."

"Oooh, I don't remember there being a roasted red potato hash on the menu."

"There isn't. Felix—oh wait, Corinne said we're all going to call him Spense—had them make it especially for you. He also sent the roses. Aren't they wonderful?"

"They are indeed. Let me get you a tip…"

"No, ma'am. Spense has taken care of everything. Is there anything else you'd like, or you'd rather have?"

"No. This looks and smells delicious. Thank you."

Saoirse tucked into her breakfast and watched the world go by outside the window on the streets below, as London came to busy life. Just as she pushed back from the table, stuffed to the gills, she felt a change in the temperature of the room. She turned in her seat, scanning her room. Sure enough, the ghost Victoria materialized through the door. The girl wore a worried expression.

"Good morning, Victoria. Can you tell me more about what happened to you? I have several friends who would like to help you and the others."

"The one who killed the other Irish witch is gone now, but the one who helped him is very angry. He doesn't want anyone to know…"

"But you and your friends are trapped, aren't you?" Saoirse asked. The ghost nodded, glancing around her as if frightened. *What the hell could frighten a ghost?*

"We're afraid of the man. He's the one who threw us away. He has kept us hidden all these years."

"My friends and I are pretty good at battling people from the other side. In fact, the man who murdered the other Irish witch escaped her trap and tried to hurt my friend, but we found a way to banish him to Hell. I'm pretty sure we could help you and your friends, but I have to know where to look for you."

"We are here," she said. "I shouldn't be talking to you," and then she repeated her riddle in her sing-song voice before disappearing.

"They did not search for those who died;
The chapel bell did not knell;
When the Irish witch can answer why,
Then our spirits will arise from Hell
And with the King of Kings we will abide."

It was a bit like Saoirse imagined talking to the Cheshire Cat might have been. Victoria slowly began dematerializing, with the last thing to go being her face. It was eerie just to see a disengaged face with no hair or other body parts before it completely vanished with the last of her words.

Where the hell were they even supposed to start? They didn't know how many souls Victoria was talking about; they didn't know where they were. They only knew these spirits were trapped and wanted to get to the Light. Anne had said the Warder could only help those who'd died at the Tower, but perhaps if they could talk to him, he could tell them who might be able to help from the other side.

She needed to ask Spense how she might contact their friend Eddy to see if he'd learned anything. And she also had to prepare the ointment Corinne and the other staff members wanted her to make for them. Knowing that the muscle-relaxing salve took some time to craft, Saoirse grabbed her bag and headed down to the lobby. She could pick up the things she needed, drop them at Rachel's and maybe even get it made before meeting Spense for lunch.

If not, she'd drop off the ingredients and take a look around Rachel's flat. If she and Spense were going to explore this new relationship, she'd need a place in London. She'd thought about it for the future and now believed it might be the time to find something permanent in the capital city.

Saoirse caught Spense's eye as he was helping some guests. He smiled and lifted his hand to wave. She did the same. As she walked out onto the Strand, one of the valets approached her.

"Ms. Madigan? Mr. Spenser has put a car and driver at your disposal."

She grinned. "Of course he has. Mr. Spenser is a very nice man that way."

The young man returned her friendly expression. "Yes, ma'am, he is. But you should know he doesn't normally do this for just anyone."

"I appreciate your loyalty to your boss. And having a car and driver would make my day so much better."

Within a few minutes, a car was brought around, and an engaging middle-aged man stepped out from behind the wheel and held her door for her. She spent the next hour visiting shops and markets, gathering the things she needed to make the salve. The driver had been of enormous help, suggesting places that might have what she needed either for less money, higher quality or both.

She got out at Rachel's place in the Charing Cross neighborhood. The building had once been a factory and Rachel's flat was on the top floor. It had high ceilings; it was an airy loft with a balcony. The open space featured a designated kitchen and luxurious bath. For Saoirse, the biggest selling features were the floor to ceiling windows on the back wall, and the gorgeous set of French doors that led out onto the balcony. Of course, the original, wide-plank wood floors, soapstone counters and exposed duct work were right up there as well. She loved it all.

It occurred to her that she had no idea where Spense lived, nor whether he wanted them to live together. Perhaps she was foolish to think he wanted to move forward quickly. On the one hand, it hadn't taken his friends any time at all to settle into their relationships, but Spense struck her as a more cautious man. It didn't matter though; she knew Rachel wanted to sell her place, and regardless of what happened between herself and Spense, Saoirse really did want a place of her own to stay when she was in London visiting her friends.

She and Rachel had maintained a close relationship since their college days, but since Rachel had moved to London they had become closer. Luckily, when Rachel became friends with Sage and later with Anne, Saoirse had been an accepted member of their inner circle. Rachel's husband, DSI Michael Holmes, had dubbed them the Hooligan Sisters, and they did their damnedest to live up to the name.

Saoirse glanced at the clock on the microwave. She had just enough time to get the liquified salve poured into the mason jars she'd purchased and set out on the kitchen island to cool before making it back to the hotel in time to meet Spense. As previously arranged, the driver was waiting for her and whisked her back to the Savoy.

She waited in the elegant lobby while Spense finished up with a guest. He walked over to her and kissed her cheek.

"I missed you," he said with a smile. "Did you have a good morning?"

"I did. Am I dressed all right for wherever we're going? Or we could go up to my room…"

He laughed. "And I wouldn't make it back to work. No, I had the catering staff put us together a picnic basket. It should be here in a minute. I thought we'd walk over to the other side of the street and find a place to eat."

"That sounds great. And by the way, breakfast was amazing and I love the roses."

"They're a bit bohemian, but then so are you, so I thought you might. But if you prefer something more traditional…"

"Never."

They collected their picnic basket and blanket, then headed out, crossed the street and looked for a place they could enjoy the food, mild weather and each other.

Once they sat down and had food dished out, Spense said, "I saw Victoria last night as I was coming up in the freight elevator. I've never heard of anyone seeing her there before."

Intrigued, Saoirse asked, "Did she say anything?"

"No. She just looked very sad and then walked through the doors before they opened. That was a bit disconcerting."

Saoirse laughed. "That's nothing. This morning when she came to my room…"

"When did that happen?"

"After you left and I had breakfast. Spense, don't be alarmed. Victoria has been part of my life on and off since I was a child. I don't believe she means anyone any harm. I just think she wants help for herself and the others who are trapped with her. The man who put them there is still a malevolent presence to her and she warned me to be careful. Then—and this is the spooky part…"

"Banshees, Jack the Ripper and a ghost aren't spooky enough for you?" he teased.

"Hardly," she scoffed. "But she started dematerializing right in front of me as she sang me her riddle. In the end, her disembodied face was all I could see."

"That must have been frightening. Why didn't you call me?"

"Because I am convinced she is no threat to any of us. And I'm used to her. Besides, she was gone. I was hoping you had heard something from Eddy."

Spense nodded. "I have, but Eddy wants to talk to you directly."

"I didn't think he was out of the books."

"He isn't. But we set up a special email, and he's been able to expand that so you can message back and forth in real time. I told him we would speak with him this evening at seven. If it was presumptuous of me…"

Saoirse took his face in her hands. "Presume away."

CHAPTER 8

Spense arranged to have Saoirse taken back to Rachel's flat in Charing Cross and picked up when she was finished making her *witch's brew*. He supposed he ought not think of it that way if they were going to build a life together. He owed it to her to be respectful of who and what she was as well as the power she could wield. Roark had been impressed with her abilities to call forth the banshees and banish a spirit as malevolent as the Ripper to Hell—and Roark was not a man easily impressed. But Spense had seen her power for himself when they had fought the Warder of the Veil and the Angel of Death.

Saoirse. Just thinking her name made him smile. She was extraordinary. Last night had been nothing short of spectacular, and she had been so responsive to his style of dominance. He had no doubt that they would lock horns. He'd seen her proud, stubborn and defiant streak, but he was sure they would find their way. It was one thing to be a training Dom in a club; it was another altogether when your heart was involved—and Spense knew his heart was most definitely involved.

Spense was glad that Saoirse knew the truth about his origins. He had often wondered how he might share that bit of information should he be so lucky as to find a woman with whom he wanted to spend his life. No one had needed to tell Saoirse; she had known and had forced the issue between Holmes and Rachel by threatening Holmes that if he didn't tell Rachel, she would. The best part was, it didn't seem to bother her at all. She had accepted him, Roark and Holmes, as well as Anne, without so much as a second thought. She was one of those people who accepted others as she found them. It was one of the things he admired most about her.

His mobile vibrated, and he pulled it from his pocket. It was Roark.

"Felix… Wait, I understand from Sage that we are now to refer to you as Spense."

Spense chuckled as he leaned back in his chair. "You really do need to ensure that she doesn't make a joke out of people's names."

"Thank God you didn't come out of the books as described. I'm not sure your beautiful witch would have succumbed to your charms quite so easily."

"Probably not. What's up?" he asked, tapping his pen on the leather desk blotter.

"Sage thought the four of us could have dinner at the Coal Hole."

"What an excellent idea. I thought dinner the other night with Holmes and Watson was outstanding."

"As did I. When I was talking to Sage about it, she reminded me that she hadn't been there in ages and suggested I call you."

Spense glanced at his watch; he knew many thought them to be out of fashion, but he was not among them. "Saoirse is over at Rachel's mixing up a batch of her salve. A number of people here swear by it, and she promised it to them. After that, we were planning to have dinner. I'm sure she'd love it if the four of us got together."

"Fine. I'll make a reservation for us at, say, six-thirty?"

"That should be fine. Saoirse should be back about six."

"Spense, for what it's worth, I think the change of name and the woman who instituted it may well be the best thing that's happened to you since we left the books."

"I couldn't agree with you more, Roark," said Spense, smiling. "Last night exceeded any and all expectations and fantasies I might have had. Don't get me wrong; I'm sure we'll have our bumps in the road like any other couple, but she is truly magnificent."

"I—actually, we—couldn't be happier for you both. Any chance she'll move here?"

Spense paused. "We haven't had a chance to talk, but I hope so," he said. "She seems fond of Rachel's flat. I'm planning to talk to Rachel about buying it when she and Holmes return. It would be much more convenient than my current place."

"It is nice. I've talked to Sage about buying a place, but she likes it here and the staff treat us so well. I do wonder if part of that isn't a bit of fear on her part."

"Could be, but I don't think we're ever going back…"

"Neither do I. Anne made the comment the other day that a trip from behind the Veil is one way—unless, of course, the Angel of Death means to drag you back through to take you to eternal darkness."

"You'd think," said Spense with a liberal dose of humor, "that being a fictional character, becoming sentient and entering the real world would be the most exciting thing that ever happened to me, but it isn't."

"I wouldn't think so. Your Saoirse is almost as glorious as my Sage."

"On that, my dear friend, we'll have to agree to disagree."

"Done. I'll call and make the reservation…"

"Let me," Spense offered. "I'm well known to the staff there. Even if they're booked, they'll find us something."

"Sounds good. We'll meet you downstairs."

Spense ended the call and texted Saoirse with the details. After she agreed it would be fun, he booked a dinner reservation for four and then went back to work, ensuring that every guest at the hotel was treated to the Savoy experience—exceptional service and accommodations.

Over the course of the afternoon, Spense found his mind drifting back again and again to Saoirse— not just the incredible night they had shared, but all the small, insignificant things that had happened. Her gentle smile, her eyes full of mischief, their comfortably intimate conversations—all of it enchanted him. For the first time, he wished he'd had a family. Before today, relatives had seemed like a nuisance that he didn't need, but right now, he would have liked to have parents to introduce her to. He supposed, in a way, the four couples had formed their own family of sorts. He found it intriguing that of the eight of them, only Watson had family and he was estranged from them. None had come to London for his wedding. Although, come to think of it, he wasn't sure they'd been invited.

Spense was quite sure that if he'd had a mother, she would have adored Saoirse. Who wouldn't? The Irish witch was strong, intelligent, beautiful and had the most amazing heart. He found her to be among the people he most admired. He also liked that while she seemed acquiescent to his dominance, she had no problem holding her own against Holmes and Roark. He was pretty sure she and Eddy would hit it off.

Shit! Eddy. They were supposed to chat at seven. That could be remedied. Taking a break, he entered his office and used the chat link Eddy had left him. The first thing he did was change his name in the chat feature.

Eddy: Spense, huh?

Spense: Yes. A bit of change. Saoirse prefers Spense and so do I.

Eddy: Especially when she's whispering it in your ear.

Spense: Knock it off, Eddy.

Eddy: Sorry. Serious?

Spense: Very. It just moved past friendship last night so it's very new. I wanted to ask if we could move our chat to tomorrow.

Eddy: I don't think that's a good idea. I'm finding some disturbing threads. We may want to bring Holmes and Roark in on it.

Spense: We're having dinner with Sage and Roark. Should I move our reservation?

Eddy: Not necessary. Why don't I give you what I have and then let you decide? I like to keep these short so I'm attaching a file. You can download it and share it with Saoirse and the others as well. Why don't you check back with me later tonight?

Spense: Sounds good. Thanks, Eddy. We're not endangering you, are we?

Eddy: Not that I know of. I just like to keep real-time interactions short.

Spense: Our reservation is at six-thirty. Why don't we check in with you about nine?

Eddy: That should work. I'll talk to you then. Congrats on your lady.

Spense: Thanks.

∽

Saoirse finished up the batch of muscle-relaxing, pain-reducing salve for those at the Savoy who had found it useful. As some of it still needed to solidify, she set the mason jars on the kitchen counter where they would sit undisturbed.

Now, she needed to make some personal plans. When she'd come for Rachel and Anne's weddings, she hadn't planned to stay indefinitely or even for an extended period of time. So, she hadn't packed much. Saoirse looked at the website for Coal Hole and decided that while most of what she'd brought would be appropriate for the restaurant, she wanted to wear something different. Something new.

She headed back to some of the stores she, Rachel and Sage had visited with Anne when shopping for her new wardrobe. She managed to find leather leggings, denim leggings and a pair of distressed jeans, as well as two new sweaters, a silk tank top and a brocade frock coat that she was sure had once been part of a costume. Saoirse was on her way out the door when she spotted a pair of hunter green suede, over-the-knee, flat boots. She looked over her shoulder at the salesperson, who smiled and nodded.

"And if you're interested, there's another silk tank that would look killer with the frock coat and the denim leggings."

"You're not helping," laughed Saoirse.

"Well, it depends on who you're referring to. Besides, you know you wanted those cinnamon jade drop earrings."

The woman had a point. The only reason Saoirse had seen the boots in the first place was that she was turning around to go back and purchase the unusual earrings she had tried to deny herself. She added the boots, which felt like heaven on her feet, the other silk tank, the earrings and an interesting necklace she'd spied at the last minute.

"I'm getting out of here before I fall in love with everything else," Saoirse called over her shoulder as she rushed back to Rachel's apartment to meet the driver Spense had sent.

There had been a time she'd thought Holmes tended to be controlling in the way he treated Rachel. But now as she approached the waiting car, she had to admit that having someone who tried to make your life easier was rather nice.

"Hey!" she called, waving to get the driver's attention.

"Ms. Madigan, you should have called and let me know to pick you up someplace else," he said as he met her and grabbed her packages.

"I had planned to be back and waiting for you, but there was a pair of killer boots that called my name."

The driver chuckled. "Do you need to go back upstairs?"

"Nope. I've got everything I need. Before I head back to Ireland, I'll need to pick up the batch of salve but I should be good."

"I know I speak for the rest of the staff when I say we hope you'll be around more often. Mr. Spenser always seems happier when you're around. Besides, watching you four ladies confound Mr. Samuels, DSI Holmes, Mr. Watson and Mr. Spenser is always such great fun."

The driver got her back to the Savoy safe and sound. She grabbed her purchases, assuring him she would have no trouble getting them up to her room. As she entered the foyer, she waggled her fingers at Spense, who was helping a younger woman with a harassed expression gather her two charges, a rambunctious set of twins, into a waiting car. Once he had passed the small group to the valets, he quickly joined her, taking all but the smallest bag from her.

"You did some shopping, I see," he said, ushering her into the lift and hitting the button for the fifth floor.

Having someone seeing to her needs and making things easier for her was something she could get used to. "You do know I am perfectly capable of carrying my purchases up to my room without assistance, don't you?"

"I do, but part of the Savoy experience is assisting our guests with the things that make staying here a true pleasure and respite. Besides, as your Dom, it is my responsibility to see that you are cared for."

"Hmm, does that mean endless orgasms?" she teased.

Spense leaned down and kissed her. "As a matter of fact, it does."

"I'm beginning to believe this whole having a Dom thing might work out for me."

"I intend to make sure you never have a reason to doubt it," said Spense. "By the way, I moved our chat with Eddy to nine, and he suggested we might want Roark and Sage with us. He sent me a report which I forwarded to Roark."

"I told you, Victoria is not a threat to me or anyone else, for that matter."

"No, sweetheart, she isn't. The girl you call Victoria is really Alice Moore, one of five young girls who went missing beginning in the late summer and early fall of 1888."

Saoirse's eyebrows shot up. "Isn't that the time of the Whitechapel murders?"

"Approximately. The five Ripper victims known as the canonical five were between August and November 1888."

"What the hell are the canonical five? You don't mean these five young girls, do you?" asked Saoirse.

"No. Not at all. But I do find it curious that the five young girls, including our ghost, went missing at roughly the same time as the five adult women that the Yard has always believed were victims of Jack the Ripper. The murders all occurred within one mile of each other. In addition to Mary Jane Kelly, the victims included Mary Ann Nichols, Annie Chapman, Elizabeth Stride and Catherine Eddowes. There is some speculation that there were six additional murders that bore some similarity to the original five, but opinion is largely divided as to whether they were victims of the Ripper or not."

"Okay, so in addition to the canonical—I love that word, by the way—five murders, five young girls went missing as well."

"Precisely. I didn't really study Eddy's report, just scanned it for salient points. I left a copy for you in your room. The girls were between the ages of five and thirteen…"

When they reached Saoirse's room, Spense used

his master code to unlock the door and then let her precede him into the room. *I could definitely get used to this.*

"And you think Victoria's real name is Alice?" Saoirse asked.

"Yes. Eddy found a picture, and the ghost looks just like her." He set the packages down gently, then turned to face her.

"I always thought she looked to be eight or nine," she mused.

"She was nine. The girls were five, seven, nine, eleven and thirteen."

"God, they were so young. Were they ever found?"

"No. And there seems to be no connection to each other, except they were orphans—which lends itself to Rachel's theory that they were wearing hand-me-downs."

"Alice?" Saoirse called quietly. "Alice?"

There was no response.

"Sweetheart? I don't know that it's a good thing that you're calling her."

"I want her to know that I know her name. I want to let her know we're going to try and help them."

Spense shook his head, kissed her and smiled. "I suppose I'm going to have to get used to you dealing in the supernatural."

Saoirse cocked her head to the side. "Says the man who stepped out of the pages of a number of novels along with his friends, one of whom fell in love with a woman who had Jack the Ripper after her and another who fell in love with and married Queen Anne Boleyn."

"Yes, that man," he said ruefully. "Before we head out, I want to go back downstairs and change."

"I thought this was the extra suit you kept downstairs."

"It is. I had one of the members of the butlering staff pick me up something more casual to wear this evening."

"But you're planning to stay with me tonight, aren't you?"

Spense cupped her head with one hand, wrapping his arm around her waist with the other and drawing her close against his body. Lowering his head, he whispered, "Banshees couldn't keep me from your bed."

CHAPTER 9

Spense made an *amuse bouche* of her mouth before leaving and telling her they were all meeting in the lobby in half an hour. After assuring him she'd be there, she closed the door behind him and hugged herself. Saoirse couldn't remember a time she'd been happier.

She unpacked her purchases and chose to wear the outfit she'd put together with the salesperson's help. Saoirse wanted to show Sage the killer hunter green boots she'd bought. She was dressed in all but the frock coat when she felt a familiar chill envelop the room.

Saoirse turned to face the space she'd last seen the ghost. "Alice?" she called gently. "I'm so sorry I didn't know your name."

The room grew even colder as Alice materialized in front of her. "The others have names too."

"I'm sure they do. I probably can even look them up in the report my friend gave me. Were you all at the same orphanage?"

"Yes. Ingram's Home for the Less Fortunate. There were boys and girls, but none of the boys were taken."

"Can I ask you about what happened?"

Alice glanced down, her small head bowed as she grabbed her skirt and seemed to twist back and forth. "We weren't supposed to talk about it, but then they decided we couldn't keep the secret." A look of fear flashed in her eyes and Saoirse wondered what might have happened that could cause a ghost to fear after all this time. "They didn't want anyone to know what happened."

"Were you all killed at the same time?" Saoirse asked gently.

"No, but in the end we were all thrown down into a hole. We were dead, but we weren't alone and we couldn't escape. We tried once, but the doctor stopped us. I'm the only one who ever leaves. I thought when we were moved, we would be able to pass on, but he trapped us here." Alice glanced around fearfully. "I have to go back."

"Alice, will you come again tomorrow?"

"I will come again but I can't say when. Time has lost its meaning. But soon."

She turned and ran toward the door, passing through it as if it were nothing. Saoirse looked at the clock, grabbed the frock coat and headed to the elevator. As the doors were about to open, a man of average height and stature stood blocking her passage. For a moment, Saoirse didn't register that he wasn't real. He glared at her before disappearing before her eyes.

She stepped into the elevator car and as the doors closed, she said quietly to the empty car, "You don't scare me, doctor, whoever you are. If I can, I will help Alice and those you sought to silence forever."

Her lift opened up on the lobby floor at the same time as Sage and Roark's.

"You look great! Is that outfit new?" asked Sage.

"You bloody well know it is," answered Saoirse.

Spense joined the trio, brushing Saoirse's lips with his. From anyone else, it might have been nothing, but Saoirse was finding Spense's attentive kindness and ability to make even the most gentle affection seem rife with sensual possibilities to be intoxicating.

The two couples left the Savoy and headed for the Coal Hole, which was part of the entire Savoy complex. Once inside, Saoirse admired its elaborate décor. The quintessentially old English pub—with its enormous bar, inlaid floors, paneled walls and open beamed ceiling—was at once elegant and casual. It was an upscale pub that had never forgotten its origins. Saoirse loved it.

Once they were seated, Spense remarked, "They say the original space was the coal cellar for the hotel, but it's also well known as a *song and supper club*. Patrons were encouraged to sing, and in Edwardian times Gilbert and Sullivan performed here regularly."

Sage nodded. "The Shakespearean actor Edmund Keane was said to have started a club for husbands whose wives wouldn't let them sing in the bath."

"Are they still taking members?" quipped Roark.

"Sweetheart, I love you to death, but you couldn't be perfect. So, you can't carry a tune even in a bucket," teased Sage.

Saoirse loved watching the two of them banter; their love was apparent even to the casual observer. The four decided to order four different main dishes—the fish and chips, the baked macaroni and cheese, the pale ale pie and a club sandwich—along with the loaded nachos and a variety of cask ales. The choice proved to be inspired as the food was delicious and no one had to eat just one thing.

Their waiter, understanding what their intent was, had everything placed in the center of their table with serving spoons and then gave each of them a separate plate. Soon they were enjoying hand-battered and deep-fried haddock, a wonderful mature cheddar sauce and pasta, the marvelous, traditional steak pie and a club sandwich that put others to shame, as well as the nachos and side dishes.

"Do you know how the club sandwich got its name?" asked Sage.

Roark groaned. "Do not encourage her; this is

what one gets when he marries a romance writer who likes to get the details right."

"Well, especially in my paranormal books, I like to ground everything in reality. The sandwich was developed in the late eighteen-hundreds in a gambling hall in Saratoga Springs, New York and is actually an acronym formed from the ingredients Chicken and Lettuce Under Bacon."

"Seriously?" said Spense. "I always thought it was the specialty of a specific club at a golf course or something like that."

"Nope," said Sage, happily. "I found that out when I was doing some research for a series I want to set in the horse racing world."

"And yet another reason I could never write a novel," said Saoirse. "I'd end up spiraling down a rabbit hole on research I find interesting but that has no relevance to anything."

Sage sipped her ale and nodded. "I know. There are days when Roark asks me how the writing went, and I have to admit nothing made the written page for a novel because I got lost following threads of research I'll never use."

Roark reached over and squeezed her hand. "That's all right, love. You do organize it all, so if you need it down the road, you have it. That's one of the reasons I think we ought to look at buying a home."

"I can't imagine our leaving the Savoy…" Sage started.

"Nothing will ever pull any of us back," said Roark, softly.

"I agree with Roark," said Spense. "We all have too much to anchor us to this world, and Anne said her understanding was that it was a one-way trip…"

"Unless Azrael wanted to drag you back," said Saoirse. "But that is my understanding as well."

"And Eddy's done quite a bit of research that confirms that," added Spense.

"Do you think he'll ever try to pierce the Veil?" asked Saoirse.

"Roark and the boys have always said no, but I'm not sure I believe that," said Sage. "I've used the message system they've set up, and I think he's developing feelings for Corinne."

"Corinne?" asked Roark. "The night concierge?"

"What's wrong with Corinne?" asked Saoirse. "I think she's nice. She's the first person who ever talked to me about Alice."

"Who's Alice?" asked Sage. "And I agree about Corrine' she's a very nice person."

"Eddy thinks that's the ghost in the Victorian dress," supplied Roark. "I don't know that Sage had time to read the report Eddy gave us, which was quite detailed."

Spense nodded. "Agreed. Saoirse and I were going to talk to him tonight, and we pushed back the time so we could meet you two for dinner first."

"Oh my God," said Saoirse. "I almost forgot to

tell you. I saw Alice earlier tonight as I was getting ready. She told me they were down in a hole and a man hurt and killed them, then they were put in the hole where they couldn't escape."

"How awful," said Sage.

"Oh, it gets better… I think I met the doctor earlier tonight."

"What?" questioned Spense. "Why didn't you say something?"

"Because when I got off, Sage and Roark were there, and I got distracted. Just before I got on the lift, this guy dressed in what I'm assuming was Victorian garb appeared before me, glared a moment and then disappeared."

"What did he look like?" asked Roark.

"About average height for a man, a bit taller than me. He was kind of fluffy, for lack of a better term. A bit overweight, but not morbidly obese—just well-fed. He had a kind of Caesar haircut and muttonchop sideburns."

"What did you do?" asked Sage.

"I told him he wasn't going to stop us from helping Alice and her friends," stated Saoirse. Roark and Spense groaned in unison. "What? We're not going to let him, are we? I'm not anyway."

"No, sweetheart, we're going to help those girls, but we don't need to throw down the gauntlet to the ghost of the guy who, at best, knows what happened and at worst, and in all likelihood, killed them."

"Roark's right. I didn't have a chance to look at Eddy's brief," said Sage. "I need you to fill me in."

"Five young girls went missing toward the end of the canonical five…" started Saoirse.

"That's the original five women in the Whitechapel murders, right?"

Saoirse nodded. "They ranged in age from five to thirteen. They went missing, according to Alice, from the same orphanage. She said none of the boys were touched, but there was a doctor involved. I believe it was the one I saw tonight."

"Were they mutilated like the Ripper's victims?"

"Unknown," said Roark. "No one ever saw the bodies. In fact, they were never reported as having been killed, just missing from Ingram's Home for the Less Fortunate."

"But the Savoy isn't in Whitechapel. Why would they be buried here?" said Sage, trying to puzzle it out.

"No, but the Savoy was being finished about the same time," offered Spense. "What better place to hide the bodies than under a new building that's being placed over an old one?"

"And why trap their spirits? Alice said he murdered them because he was afraid they would tell. Tell what, I have no idea, but they were killed to keep them quiet. Yet who could they tell in the afterlife? By now, anyone who was alive then would be dead too."

"Unless it was someone famous," offered Sage.

"Someone whose reputation might be damaged; someone they didn't want associated with scandal."

"So, not only do we need to find out all about these girls," said Saoirse, "we need to find out about the doctor and who he was trying to protect."

Glancing at the Rolex on his wrist, Roark said, "Then I suggest we order dessert to go and take it back to the Savoy so we can plan while we eat. I say we order one each of the Belgian chocolate brownie and apple pie and two of the sticky toffee puddings."

"Agreed," said Spense, "but tell them we'll heat them at home and get our own ice cream."

Once they'd gathered their things and paid the bill, they made their way back to the hotel. It was nice walking arm-in-arm with Spense. Saoirse noticed that both he and Roark walked on the street side so that she and Sage were in a more protected position. It made her smile.

As they got into the lift, Sage pushed the button for the floor with their suite. "I have bigger monitors and a better desk set-up, but we can go…"

Saoirse stayed her hand before she could push the button for the fifth floor. "I think that sounds like the right thing to do."

When they entered the room, the difference in temperature between the hallway and the room itself was easily discernible.

"Alice?" whispered Saoirse as she entered the room.

The entire room shook as the Doctor materialized before their eyes. He wore a light brown wool suit and white broadcloth shirt, both in the Victorian style. Sage and Saoirse were pushed back by Roark and Spense, who stood protectively in front of them.

"You will not meddle in things which don't concern you," the specter intoned.

Saoirse pushed past Spense. "But it does concern me…"

Spense took hold of her arm, trying to draw her back. "Saoirse, stay behind me."

"If he was of this world, maybe, but he isn't," she said, pulling free and facing the ghost.

"You would do well not to cross me, woman," warned the specter.

"That's your second mistake. I'm not just a woman—I'm a witch. You want to try and intimidate me? It's going to take more than shaking the room." She turned her head to address her friends. "Trust me, he doesn't have the power to shake the hotel."

Muttering a spell under her breath, the floor beneath them seemed to vibrate and the specter took a step back.

"Yeah," said Saoirse. "Two can play at that game. Want to know what your first mistake was? I'll tell you… murdering those girls. We're going to find them and set their spirits free. If you can, I suggest you make your way to the other side and make your case to the powers that be. I banished one evil spirit to Hell; I can banish yours as well."

"Witch," he sneered.

"You got that right," Saoirse said as she gathered energy in a ball in front of her and pushed it at the Doctor, who vanished in an instant. Feeling pleased with herself, Saoirse turned to face her friends as the floor ceased shaking. Both Roark and Spense looked pissed… and not at the ghost. "Problem?"

"Big time," whispered Sage.

"We'll discuss it after we speak with Eddy," said Spense.

CHAPTER 10

Sage fired up her system. She never left it running if she wasn't going to be in their suite. It was her lifeline to her work and to all the stories she had left to write, and she didn't want to risk it getting fried by a power surge.

"That guy looked so familiar," said Sage, trying to break the awkward silence.

"From where?" asked Saoirse, who had a dreadful feeling that she was about to experience discipline firsthand.

Sage took the desserts from Roark, who was opening the ice cream the staff had delivered to their room, packed in ice. One of the advantages of living at the hotel was the ability to call ahead so something was waiting for you when you arrived.

"I got vanilla bean and peppermint. I thought the peppermint would be great with the brownie. As for the Doctor, I don't know. It's like I've seen his picture somewhere, as he was photographed doing something. I wish we could see Eddy when we talk, like, do a video chat."

"Why, love?" asked Roark. "You know what he looks like. After all, you created him."

"I know, but it would just be nice to put a face to the picture I have created in my mind."

As they got the desserts ready, Saoirse was beginning to believe that Spense was no longer angry.

Sage leaned into her and whispered, "Don't you believe it. He's just being very English and not making a scene. Trust me, you're looking at discipline…"

"And so will you be if you try to interfere. You know better, Sage," said Roark, "I don't want to have to tell you again."

Before anyone could say anything else. The screen blipped on.

Eddy:Hey guys. Did all of you get a chance to read my brief?

Sage:How do you know it's not just Spense and Saoirse? Oh, duh, the handle. And I didn't, but I think everyone else did and they filled me in. Saoirse was able to confirm that the little girl ghost is Alice, and we've now had a visit from another older male ghost.

Eddy:Interesting that you mention him. The brief really only talked about the five missing girls. In order of disappearance and decreasing in age, we have: Molly Thompson, aged 13; Eugenia Cook, aged 11; Alice Moore, aged 9; Louisa Shaw, aged 7; and Irene Brailey, aged 5.

Sage:Eddy, it's Saoirse. Alice is the ghost here at the Savoy. She says that she and the others were taken from Ingram's Home for the Less Fortunate. I think something happened to them and then they were killed to keep them from talking.

Eddy:That would make some sense. The older male ghost…

Sage:We've dubbed him the Doctor.

Eddy:You have no idea how accurate that moniker might be. So, he looks to be later middle age, same era, muttonchop sideburns? Looks like this?

A picture flashed up on the screen. If that wasn't their ghost, it was his
identical twin.

Sage:That's the guy. Who is he?

Eddy:Dr. William Gull, one of Queen Victoria's physicians and one she made a baronet after he successfully treated her grandson, Prince Albert Victor—supposedly for typhoid, although there are some historians who think it might have been for an STD. He was involved in the Cleveland Street scandal of 1889.

Sage:Sage again. Wasn't that a homosexual bordello?

Eddy:Yes. There was a big raid, and two nobles were caught. One of them hired a lawyer who was said to have implicated the prince, so the crown shut down the investigation. There were lots of rumors, theories and speculation about the Queen's grandson.

Sage: Roark here.

Eddy: It doesn't really matter. I figure you're all reading over each other's shoulders.

Sage: So, you think Gull was knighted for curing Prince Albert Victor of an STD?

Eddy: Not just any STD, syphilis—only it was incurable. Although there were some pretty nasty things that were supposed to cure it.

Sage: Saoirse. Are you talking about *Virgin Cleansing?*

Eddy: The timeline fits... Look, that's all I have at the moment. Tomorrow at six-thirty?

The screen blipped off

"What's got him so spooked?" Spense asked Roark.

"More than usual? Who knows? Eddy's always been spooked," answered Roark.

"No, but this isn't the first time he's jumped off without warning..."

"If we're putting him in some kind of jeopardy..." Sage broke off her thought, looking between Roark and Spense. Beside her, Saoirse dished pieces of the desserts into plates, then handed them to Sage, who scooped out the ice cream. They passed the dessert to the men, then took their own plates and sat, thinking about what they'd learned.

Spense shook his head at Sage's unspoken worry. "Doubtful," he said firmly. "I know how you wrote him, but Eddy has never lacked for courage or loyalty to his friends. If anything, he thinks he's putting us in jeopardy."

"That would make more sense," said Roark, nodding.

"Maybe whatever power it is that controls these things has realized he's sentient, which was the first step in your piercing the Veil," speculated Sage. "Or maybe he's worried that if he helps us, he'll find himself outside the book like Holmes and Spense."

"Perhaps. That certainly makes sense. Eddy doesn't want to come out," said Roark.

"I don't know that that's true anymore," said Sage.

"Why do you say that, love?"

"Corinne? Remember?" answered Sage.

"You think she's in danger too?" asked Saoirse.

"Doubtful, but it that changes, Eddy might be compelled to come out," Spense said. "But if he does have feelings for Corinne and they continue to grow, he might push to get out as well. Holmes and I have no clue how we got here, but Roark got here because Sage was in danger, and he just pushed through, but I think eventually he would have gotten through based on the strength of his feelings for Sage. The fact that we're on to the doctor and that something happened to those girls, might push him over the edge and try to do more than shake a room. He might be afraid that we're going to put an end to his reign of terror over the girls' ghosts."

"But someone was trying to kill me," said Sage. "Who would try to kill Corinne? I swear, her life is as dull as mine was before I started writing."

Saoirse shook her head. "I'm not sure Corinne is as dull as she wants us to believe, but that's a matter for another day."

"Indeed," said Spense. "Saoirse, what's a *Virgin Cleansing*?"

"It's a crackpot theory that was popular for a long time, including during the Reign of Queen Victoria," Saoirse explained. "If a man had an STD, it was believed he could be *cured* if he raped a virgin. No one called it rape, but that's what it was as I'm pretty damn sure none of them gave consent. The worst part is that even today there are *natural healers* in some third world countries who propound the theory and believe it can cure HIV/AIDS. The incidence of child rape in that part of the world is staggering."

"Surely no one believes that," scoffed Spense.

"No one with a medical degree, but a lot of people with limited understanding of these diseases are desperate to cure themselves."

"That could explain the descending ages of the girls, and the fact that they all came from the same area, and Gull trying to cover it up," mused Sage.

Saoirse shook her head, saddened. "But worse

than that, if the prince was involved in the Whitechapel murders or the disappearance of those girls, the royal family must have had knowledge of what was going on."

"More than that," Roark said, "when the prince died, they could have covered it up. And they would have wanted to ensure that no one ever knew—especially if Prince Albert Victor died of syphilis and not of typhoid or pneumonia, which are the two more prominent stories."

Spense set his dish on the coffee table. "It would also explain why the doctor was knighted. Victoria didn't hand out a lot of knighthoods. I don't think that I recall any of her other physicians being knighted for service to the crown."

"Let me get this straight," said Sage. "You all are suggesting that this Dr. Gull took these young girls for Queen Victoria's grandson to systematically rape in order to cure his STD? No wonder we Americans kicked your skanky asses to the curb in 1776."

"As I recall, when we were dealing with the Ripper, I came across the theory that Prince Albert Victor either was the Ripper himself or maybe killed the other six women who were killed in a similar fashion for the next year or two," said Saoirse. "The theory was that the syphilis drove him insane and thus he became a serial killer. There's another theory, not as well accepted, that Gull was the Ripper."

"But what if it was the Prince, and Gull was just trying to cover it up?" asked Spense.

"Surely, you're not suggesting the crown condoned such a thing?" scoffed Roark. The other three all looked at him with raised eyebrows. "Ok, maybe not so farfetched."

"If Queen Victoria knew, she most likely didn't know the specifics—the nobility and especially royalty didn't want to know the dirty details. They just wanted the problem to go away. Maybe she thought Gull just made it easier on the family by helping the prince to the other side?"

Those who were still standing sank down onto the other seats in the room.

"Is it just me or is this all starting to make a lot of sense?" asked Saoirse.

"It's monstrous, but it's the best possible theory. Prince Albert Victor was either the Ripper himself or some kind of copycat…" Sage tapped her fork on her plate, thinking it through. "Even if you believe there were eleven Ripper murders, they ended in February of 1891 and the prince died in January of 1892."

"It would also explain why the Doctor is suddenly making himself known," agreed Spense. "We're the ones who sent the Ripper to Hell. He might be figuring if anyone could bring this to light, it's us. If he killed, or helped to kill, or even covered it up, he might not have crossed over. He may have stuck around. And now, he's worried we'll expose all of this."

"Oh lord," sighed Roark, "just what we need… another vengeful spirit wanting to do one or more of us in."

∾

After dessert, Spense escorted Saoirse to the room, opening her door and allowing her to enter. But rather than following her, he stopped at the threshold.

"Saoirse…"

She turned back to look at him. "I know. You're pissed that I got in Gull's face. But if he did even half of what we think he did, the man's a monster."

"And one we have no idea how to fight. So, yes, I am concerned that you needlessly put yourself in danger…"

"You were in just as much danger as I was. At least I'm used to dealing with magickal things…"

Spense frowned at her. "I am one of those magickal things…"

Saoirse stepped toward him, grabbing his shirt and standing on her tiptoes to brush her lips against his. "I thought we dealt with one another rather well last night."

He eyed her. "We did, but if we're moving our relationship from friendship to romantic, we need to come to an understanding…"

"We had one night, Spense. An amazing night that could be the start of something wonderful, but we're moving kind of fast. I live in Ireland, and your life is here at the Savoy in London."

"I'm not trying to rush you into anything, but last night… Well, you can't unring a bell," he said. "All I could think about was getting you back into bed, getting between your legs and having at you. If this isn't what you want, I can go back to being friends, but I can't—or rather won't—do friends with benefits."

"I wouldn't ask you to do something that would make you uncomfortable."

He shook his head. "As I said, I can take a step back, but I either need to step away or step forward into the future with you at my side."

"My life is in Ireland. I draw my strength from that place."

"Strength? You mean your power is tied to Ireland?" he asked, confused.

"No. I can cast a spell anywhere, but I've built a life there—a business."

He crossed his arms, studying her. "Do people come to your farm for treatment or to pick things up?"

"Rarely. I really don't like people coming to the farm. Most of my business is done by mail order."

"So, you could move your business here if you wanted."

She shrugged. "Maybe, but I'm used to living the way I want. The one time I tried to be part of a partnership, I ended up giving up everything and almost lost myself."

"Sweetheart, I don't want *you* to lose you, but *I* don't want to lose you either."

Saoirse frowned at him, clearly frustrated. "Can't we just slow things down?"

Ah, he thought. She didn't understand. He needed to be clearer. "I can't," he explained. "I can't be in some kind of holding pattern. I know asking you to make a choice doesn't seem fair."

"At least we agree on that," she said. "Just come inside and come to bed, Spense. You aren't the only one who thought about a repeat of last night."

As much as he didn't want to refuse, he knew he had to. So, he shook his head. "I think you should think about what you want. I don't have all the answers, but if we want to be together, we can figure it out. I'm not your ex, Saoirse…"

"I didn't think you were…"

"But you want me to pay for the debts he still owes you. Our going to bed tonight won't do anything to resolve things, but maybe not having me here will help you figure it out."

"In other words, it's your way or the highway."

He reached up, cupping the nape of her neck and pulling her forward to gently kiss her. "Not at all. I'm simply telling you how I feel and where I stand. I don't want to coerce or seduce you. I want you to enter this relationship with your eyes wide open. To that end, if we go forward, I'm going to discipline you…"

"For confronting Gull?"

He shook his head. "No. For not getting behind me when I told you to. I understand the instinct to take on something that's threatening my friends. I might have scolded you later for that, but when I tell you to do something, I expect you to do it, especially in a dangerous situation. You can tell me once the danger has passed that I was being overprotective or that you aren't happy with me, but I expect you to obey." He kissed her again. "Think about what you want, Saoirse. Don't forget to engage the night latch."

Taking a deep breath, he turned and walked toward the elevators.

"Spense?" she called, running to catch up with him. He stopped, looking down at her earnest expression.

"You want honesty?" she asked "Well, I don't know what's going to happen. I don't know if I can be the woman you want and need me to be, but I do know I want to try."

CHAPTER 11

Spense scooped her up in his arms and strode back to her room, using her feet to push open the door so he could carry her in. Saoirse reached behind them and closed the door. Spense turned so she could flip the night latch. Then, he carried her to the bedroom and set her on her feet.

"I want to make sure you know what you're agreeing to," he said softly.

She nodded solemnly. "I do. I want to try and make this work with you. I don't know that I believe it will, but I know that if I don't try, I will regret it the rest of my life. And I'm not willing to risk that."

"I won't lie to you. I do want you to lose yourself in me, but I want to lose myself in you as well."

She placed her hands on either side of his head, pulling his head down. "That sounds like a fair trade," she said, her brogue deepening, before she fused her mouth to his, running her tongue along the seam of his lips.

Spense kissed her deeply, allowing his tongue to slide into her mouth, feeling her go soft and submissive. He pulled back and turned her away from him, sliding the frock coat off her shoulders and hanging it up in the closet.

Then he crossed back to the bed and sat down on the edge. "I want you naked when I discipline you, Saoirse."

"No way we can skip that part and get to the endless orgasms?"

"Look inside yourself. Is that what you really want?"

He watched a myriad of emotions play across her face before she shook her head. "No. No, it's not. Can you help me with my boots?"

She placed her foot between his spread legs, a tempting delight if there ever was one. Spense grasped her boot and pulled it off before doing the same with the other one. Saoirse walked to the closet and removed her clothes before turning back to him. Spense patted his thigh, saying nothing. When she rejoined him and offered her hand, he guided her over his thigh so that she was easily balanced over his leg, with her upper body resting on the bed. He closed his other leg against the back of her thighs, placed his left hand between her shoulder blades to hold her in place and gently caressed her buttocks with his right hand.

"So beautiful and so reckless," he murmured, his voice thick with his desire for her. "You had no idea how Gull was going to react to being confronted, especially by a woman, and a witch at that. You need to learn there are consequences when you don't follow your instinct and bend to my will."

He could feel the tension in her body. Spense knew part of it was from the anticipation of being spanked. He also knew that part was the confrontation with Gull and knowing they were committed to helping the children who had been murdered and trapped somewhere in the Savoy.

Saoirse trembled. "I'm sorry, Spense. I'll try to do better next time."

"I know you will," he said.

She wasn't the only one who needed this; he did too. He needed to know she could learn to trust that he would take care of her—and that included disciplining her when she required it. He needed to know that when push came to shove, she would mind him. He indulged himself by running his hand over her rounded globes, enjoying how silky her skin felt to the touch and looking forward to it turning a lovely shade of pink.

Spense raised his hand and brought it back down with a loud smack that echoed in the room. Saoirse moaned softly. *Good.* He began to spank her with an easy rhythm—not too fast, not too harshly, but hard enough to impart a lasting sting. He peppered her backside, ensuring he covered it evenly. She squirmed in discomfort, but she didn't try to escape his discipline.

He continued to spank her, his hard cock pressed against her belly. He tried to memorize everything about this first time. He wanted it to be special… to have meaning… to be burned into his memory in the same way as he'd always remember the first time he'd pressed himself up into her wet heat.

The change in her body as he continued to spank her was incredibly arousing. He could smell her desire, see her skin flush and her bottom turning the loveliest shade of red. For a moment, he stopped, running his finger along the inside of her thigh. With a soft cry of longing, she parted her legs. Yes, his little witch liked her spanking and was responding just the way he wanted. He brought his hand back up and cracked it across her ass, watching the place he struck redden before fading and becoming pink.

Over and over he smacked her bottom, sending heat and pain surging through her body. She moaned in response.

"When I tell you to get behind me, you bloody well get behind me, do you understand?" he asked as he continued to spank her.

"Yes, sir," she cried.

He lost track of how many times he swatted her. That didn't really matter. He was prepared to spank her as many times as it took to feel her give over. The number wasn't important, nor was the color of her backside; he needed her to relax and accept. He needed to feel the barriers drop so they could connect. He'd felt that connection last night as he'd made love to her, but this morning the walls had returned—not as rigid as before, but there, nonetheless.

The moment her body became soft and acquiescent, he stopped and pulled her up into his arms and onto his lap. He brought his mouth down on hers hard, his tongue snaking in deep and demanding her surrender. Her arms wrapped tightly around him, her nipples rubbing against his shirt. With one arm, he held her close; with the other hand, he delved between her legs. Her thighs parted easily, allowing him access to her pussy. Now she was squirming with desire. Saoirse enjoyed physical affection, which was good. He meant to see she got a lot of it.

Spense turned with her, pressing her down into the bed. She winced as her bottom hit the mattress, but then smiled when she realized he'd seen it. Her legs parted of their own accord, and the smell of her arousal assailed his nostrils. She was ripe and ready for him. The spanking had done its job, not only inflicting his discipline but preparing her for his possession.

He rolled off her and walked to the closet, removing his clothes and hanging them beside hers. Spense liked seeing them there, waiting eagerly for him. He stalked back to the bed and stretched out on top of her, making a place for himself as he shoved his cock up inside her in a single, long push. Her pussy contracted all along his length, pulling him in. God, he loved the way she felt.

Dragging himself back until only the head of his shaft was inside her sheath, he thrust in again, hard. She moaned. When he repeated the move, Saoirse embraced him, her nails digging into his back.

"God, yes. Fuck me, sir."

"You will learn to obey me, Saoirse."

"Yes, sir," she moaned as he began to fuck in and out of her.

His hands slipped beneath her body, grasping her heated globes to hold her still while he pounded into her. He groaned as he increased the speed and strength of his thrusting. Harder and harder he drove into her, slamming into her until her back bowed and she arched her entire body into his, crying out and clinging to him. Her inner walls clenched, and her entire body shook as he continued to hammer her pussy.

Her breathing sped up, becoming ragged and thready as her body raced with his toward an ecstasy he had known only with her. He plunged into her again and again, her pussy clamping down hard, until finally he slammed into her one last time. She screamed in pleasure as she writhed beneath him. Spense felt his own orgasm wash over him as he held himself hard against her, flooding her pussy with his cum, her sheath rhythmically spasming as it milked his dick for every last drop.

He collapsed on top of her, letting her take his weight. "I need to know you will be safe," he murmured as he gave her butterfly kisses all over her face. "I don't know what I'd do without you."

"I'm sorry I didn't do what you told me, and I'm even sorrier I scared you…"

He raised his head, looking down at her and smoothing her hair away from her face. "But?"

"But I may not always be able to let you take the hit. When it's supernatural, I'm probably the best one to assume the lead."

Spense shook his head. "Not necessarily. I know you might well be the only one of us who has the skill and ability to actually fight this thing or call the banshees or cast a spell, but you can bloody well do it with me standing between you and whatever it is. I don't want to stop you or limit what you can do, but I need you to let me keep you safe while you're doing it. Agreed?"

He loved watching her think. He might not yet always be able to tell what was going through her mind, but he could tell when she was considering something he'd said.

Saoirse nodded. "I think I can agree with that, but just keep in mind, I've been dealing with this kind of thing most of my life, so I may not see something as dangerous as you do. I'll give you that Gull and the Ripper were both malevolent forces, but Alice is not. She's lost—most likely trapped with those other girls. We need to find them and help them to the Light."

"Do you know how to do that?" he said as he rolled off her and raised her up to sit next to him, leaning back against the pillows.

"No, but I brought a couple of books with me—ones I won't leave when I'm away from the farm. I'll start looking through them to see what I can find. If you see Alice before I do, try and confirm that the others with her are the other four girls. A lot of times, knowing a spirit's name can help you help them or even give you a limited amount of control over them."

"I'm going to ask Roark if he minds if Sage does some research regarding any information about the missing girls."

"What about the prince and Gull?" she asked.

"I think we're better off letting Eddy do that on the dark web. How are you feeling?"

Saoirse gave him a sweet smile. "My ass hurts, but the pain is offset by the incredible feeling of peace and happiness I find lying here in your arms. Spense, can we talk about this room? I can't stay here."

"Are you afraid of Gull?" he asked, hugging her tight.

"Not really. I got a feeling of darkness from him, but not all that strong. And before you ask, not Alice. It's a matter of money." She gestured to the luxury around her. "In case you missed it, this grand hotel of yours is expensive."

"Sweetheart, your room is comped, but I hear what you're saying."

"I've been thinking about asking Rachel about buying her old flat in Charing Cross or maybe renting it."

He looked down at her and placed a lazy kiss on her lips. "I was going to ask her the same. My place is about half that size and further away… What do you say we rent it? And then we can figure out who should buy it."

"After tonight, I was thinking maybe we might buy it together."

"I like the way you think."

He cuddled her close to his side and smiled when she nestled against him and gave a sated sigh. Saoirse might not know what she wanted, but he damn sure did. When he hadn't been looking, he'd fallen deeply in love with the beautiful witch who slept at his side. He loved everything about her. The way she responded to him—be it discipline or pleasure. Her ferocity in the face of things that would terrify others.

Her compassion for a lost little girl and the ones with her who had been damned to spend eternity adrift.

Saoirse was right. They would figure out where the girls' bodies were and find a way to help their spirits move on. If what they believed had been done to them was the truth, their deaths would have been horrific, and the very least they deserved was peace and the rest of eternity in the Light.

CHAPTER 12

Spense leaned over and kissed her. Saoirse hoped he was going to pull her beneath him again. She liked being beneath Spense, feeling surrounded by his warmth. She loved the way he took her repeatedly throughout the night. He was a strong and virile lover, and she'd have to remember to thank Sage for creating him.

She reached for him and felt clothing. It was still dark out. "Stay," she mumbled. "Again."

He chuckled. His voice was like liquid chocolate in those silly wedding fountains. Maybe they should have one of those. *Wait. Wedding? Where had that come from?*

"I can't, sweetheart," he said softly, gently. "I need to go home, get a shower and get back for work. I should be back before you wake up. Call me, and I'll arrange for your breakfast."

She felt herself pouting. "For the record? I dislike you leaving this early for appearances' sake."

"What if I keep several suits down in my office, as well as some casual clothes until we can talk to Rachel and Holmes?"

"Okay. Spense?" He stopped as she sat up, allowing the covers to pool in her lap. "I want you to know I really am sorry I frightened you and that I was a chicken-shit about us. I want this. I want you. I'm crazy about you, Felix Spenser."

He grinned. "That's good. Because I'm madly in love with you."

Before she could react, he'd left her suite. She wanted to be angry that he hadn't given her time to respond, but she couldn't manage it. She drew her knees up to her chest and hugged them to her. Smiling, she flopped back down on her back and squealed with pure happiness.

Felix Spenser loved her. She'd have to make sure she told him the same. And then she'd have to endure Sage, Anne and Rachel's teasing. She'd gone and done precisely what the three of them had done—fallen in love with a wildly dominant man.

∽

When the phone woke her later that morning, it was Sage.

"I hope I didn't wake you…" she started.

Glancing at the clock on the bedside table, Saoirse groaned. She never slept this late.

"Only sort of, but I should have been up long before now."

Sage laughed softly. "You probably ought to think about taking it easy. Roark is off meeting with a new client, and I was thinking of going out for breakfast. Want to join me?"

"Absolutely, and I can be ready to go in no time. Let me call Spense and let him know. He was going to have breakfast sent up."

"He didn't stay the night?" Sage asked.

"He did, but had to leave early so he could go home, change and get back here."

"I'm starving. Can you meet me in half an hour?"

"Ugh. But make it forty-five minutes and I'm all yours." Saoirse ended the call and immediately called down to Spense's desk.

"Good morning, beautiful," he answered. Just the sound of his warm voice made her grin.

"Good morning to you too. And by the way, no fair making declarations of love and then leaving the premises."

"You're right. That was a cowardly thing to do, and you deserve better. But it doesn't change the fact that it's true."

"Not to worry," teased Saoirse, "I'll think of a way for you to make it up to me. Sage wants to go to breakfast and I'm meeting her downstairs. I'll see you in a few minutes."

She ended the conversation and dressed quickly, putting on minimal makeup and pulling her winter-wheat hair back in a loose French braid. Leaving her hotel room, she smiled as the elevator doors opened to reveal Sage already standing in the lift.

"Perfect timing," Sage greeted her.

"Do you know when Rachel and Anne will be back?"

"The end of this week, I think, but it might be next week. Do you think we need them?"

"Honestly, I don't know," Saoirse admitted. "Rachel is handy to have around for historical stuff, and I want to talk to Anne about the Void. After all, she's the only one who's been there."

"I doubt the Warder will help us, and I don't think it's safe to engage Azrael."

Saoirse shook her head. "I don't know. He may well have information we need. I know the Warder said that they couldn't come after Anne again, but I'd rather not have Azrael looking to see if he can't somehow drag Anne into the Darkness."

Sage waved her hand. "Gabe won't let her anywhere near the Tower anyway. He told Roark he doesn't trust either of them."

"Can you blame him?" Saoirse said as the doors opened.

They exited the elevator and, seeing Spense was

busy with guests, Saoirse blew him a kiss as she and Sage left the hotel in search of breakfast.

∼

June 1889
London, England

"Come along, lads," said the venerable physician. "We don't have much time. Construction has come along much faster than we thought."

"This is a gruesome business, Dr. Gull," said Lord Arthur Somerset, a man who was known to have loose morals. To hear him call something gruesome was surprising. But the doctor paid little heed.

"That is not your concern," he said.

"Really, Gull, I think there are others better suited to this kind of manual labor," said the Earl of Euston.

Dr. Gull, who had been born of modest family origins, stopped and held the lantern up so he could see these wealthy lords who were so busily judging him. "And do you think Her Majesty would entrust this business to those she has no reason to trust or who don't have their own compelling reasons to keep their mouths shut?"

Both noblemen were silent.

"Well, then, let's get on with it," said Somerset.

They were right. This was a gruesome business, but it had to be done. Richard D'Oyly Carte's new hotel was being built on the site of the Savoy Palace built in 1246 and would open within the next few months.

"The palace that once stood here had an oubliette."

"What the hell is that?" asked Somerset.

"An oubliette is a dungeon where the only access is through a trapdoor in its ceiling. We can lay them to rest there. They will be sealed within their grave, and no one will know," said Gull.

The Earl frowned. "I take it the cure didn't work?"

Gull shook his head. "I'm afraid not. Even the youngest of them had no effect. I fear we waited too long to try the cure, and the ravages of the disease have taken the Prince's mind."

"The city is rife with rumor that the prince may well be the Ripper," said Somerset.

"Not possible. The Queen has vouched for his whereabouts…"

"Well, she would, wouldn't she?" scoffed the Earl.

They stopped the darkened carriage, ensuring there was no one nearby to see what they were about to do. Gull went around to the trade entrance of the hotel site. Using a key given to him by a member of the Queen's staff, he opened the door and the three men carried in the bodies of five little girls—ages thirteen to five. They laid down their burdens, sewn into linen body bags, and removed the subflooring until they found the trap door and opened it.

Gull had wondered about the thirteen-year-old Molly Thompson. Girls of that age and with her background and no family were known to be promiscuous. The same could be said of Eugenia Cook. But he'd really believed Alice Moore, Louisa Shaw or Irene Bailey would provide the cure to the prince's syphilis. But he feared they'd been too late. The prince was descending further and further into madness and becoming more and more violent.

After killing the girls, Gull had spread a special blessed salt over them that would keep a soul from escaping its mortal coil before wrapping them in canvas bags. The man who'd sold it to him had assured him it could stop a vampire from rising. After lowering the bodies into the oubliette, Gull salted the makeshift grave again before filling the hole with rock and dirt they'd found, closed the trap door and reinstalled the subflooring. They stopped when they heard the creaking of footsteps overhead. The impresario had hired guards to look after the almost complete luxury hotel, but there was no reason for them to go to the service entrance or come down here into the basement.

As the footsteps faded away, the men made their way back to their carriage, careful to lock up behind them and leave no trace of ever having been there. They made their way back to their meeting place, and the Earl of Euston and Lord Somerset got out of the carriage.

"You have been of great service to Her Majesty and the crown," said Gull. "It will not be forgotten. I would remind you to never speak of this to anyone. Should you ever find yourself in need of Her Majesty's favor, simply hand someone in authority a piece of paper with the letters P-A-V. Any mention of this night's events outside the three of us will be cause for you to be accused of treason."

With that, Dr. Gull got back into the carriage and took it to the site where he meant to dispose of it before making his way back home.

∼

January 1890
London, England

Gull hadn't been feeling well. He'd suffered several strokes, which his own physicians felt were brought on by age, bad diet, and exhaustion, but Gull knew better. He was being scared to death. Twice now in the last several months, he swore he saw the ghost of Alice Moore. The ghost would say nothing and make no aggressive move toward him. She would simply stand there in her yellow dress and stare accusingly at him.

He often wondered if being killed and buried in a grave no one would ever know about had caused their spirits to remain trapped somewhere between Heaven and Hell. And perhaps this ghostly apparition was the proof of it.

This morning, she had appeared again just as he headed downstairs for breakfast.

His valet, who was in close attendance, realized something was amiss and helped him to his sitting room. Sir William sat down and wrote on a piece of paper: "I have no speech." The valet summoned his family and helped Sir William back to his bedroom. He was attended by three close associates, Dr. Weber, Dr. Hood and Dr. Acland, who watched over him as he slipped into unconsciousness and then into death.

Sir William's spirit rose above the bed, and he looked down on the scene. His family and doctors had stayed by his side as he'd passed away. He was pleased to see the procession of carriages that had drawn up to the door with people making inquiries as to his state of health. The Prince of Wales, and most likely Her Majesty, had been kept informed of his condition.

Sir William could not see the Light, nor feel the presence of his loved ones who had gone before him. Instead, he saw the Angel of Death in a dark hooded cloak with a long-handled scythe in his hand. The specter pointed his skeletal finger at the doctor, who walked away.

No! He was not ready to go. He still had his duty to perform. He had to ensure that there was no way those five little girls could cast the light of suspicion on the prince, even from their grave. So far, he'd been able to keep their souls trapped in that dark place, but he needed to ensure that they remained silent forever. He had promised Queen Victoria he would guard the secret with his last breath and beyond, until the danger to Prince Albert Victor was eradicated.

∼

Present Day
London, England

"Do you think we're going to be able to help those girls?" asked Sage as she bit into a buttery English muffin. They headed to one of the local cafes that served breakfast. Sage sometimes came here to write and the staff knew her well. She'd been shown to her usual table that was somewhat private but had a great view of the rest of the restaurant.

"I have to believe it. I just think we need to figure out what happened, where they were dumped…"

"Why do you say dumped, Saoirse? Wasn't there a chapel in the original Savoy Palace? Couldn't they have been buried there? And why more than a century later do we need to know why they were killed?"

"Because Alice told us we did. No one searched for her or the others with her. At this point, we're just assuming that it's the other missing girls. She flat out says, *when the Irish witch can answer why*, then their spirits can rise from where they are and go into the Light."

"Any idea how we figure it out and then make it known to the public?"

"I don't know that it will ever need to be made public or adjudicated, but I think they just need to know they weren't forgotten. Perhaps Gull is the only thing keeping them there."

Sage sat back in her chair. "Do you think so? Do you think that's why he's making threatening appearances?"

"I'd bet my life on it," said Saoirse with conviction.

CHAPTER 13

Saoirse and Sage hailed a cab and headed over to Rachel's old flat. Saoirse reminded herself that she was going to need to resign herself to London traffic. Everything seemed to take three times as long to get to as she thought it should. Traffic in London was horrendous, especially when compared to the quiet country roads she was used to. Rural Ireland was a far cry from the bustling city of London, but more and more she felt this was where she belonged.

"I love this place," said Sage as she bustled about the apartment, helping Saoirse put things back in their place and ensuring it was neat and tidy.

Saoirse nodded. "Me too. I'm going to ask her about buying it or at least leasing it."

"You're moving to London? That would be amazing, especially if Watson and Anne move back to the States."

"Why would they do that?"

"I don't think he's told anyone but Roark, so please don't say anything. Watson doesn't feel Anne is safe here, and his old unit is coming together to form a security, intelligence gathering and K&R firm. If they move, you might want to think about their place in Soho. It's a little further from the Savoy, but it's a lot bigger."

"I know, and it has that weird little area he uses for an office that would be great to use for my business. It has such tall ceilings—not that these aren't, but seriously, if I put shelving all the way up in Anne's place, I could have one of those rolling library ladders. I've always wanted one of those things. Thanks for the heads-up. Part of me thinks I should talk to Spense, and the other part says, this is all so new and we don't know where it's going. Regardless of what happens with Spense, I wanted to get a permanent place in London."

"Listen to the part that says you and Spense are going to be together." She patted Saoirse's hand, then sighed. "I'm suddenly kind of sad at all the changes. I've loved living at the Savoy, but Roark thinks we need to look at other housing options. I'm just so spoiled by the staff there. By the way, Roark and I think it's great you and Spense are going to make a go of it."

Saoirse laughed. "What Roark probably said was, it was time we both got our heads out of our asses."

"True enough, but Roark just wants his friends to be happy. And he is convinced that unless a man has a woman he's madly in love with, life isn't worth living. I have to tell you, I agree."

Saoirse dropped her eyes. "Me too. I had convinced myself that it just wasn't going to happen for me in this lifetime. And then Spense came along."

"You love him." Sage wasn't asking; she was stating a fact.

"I do. He told me this morning that he's in love with me. After he left, I kept waiting to be terrified, and it just didn't happen. All I could feel was happy, like things were finally falling into place."

"And he already knows you're a powerful witch…"

Saoirse mused as she sipped her tea. "You have no idea how complicated that can make things. Men are either intimidated, don't believe, or wonder how they can turn it to their advantage. For Spense, it's just one facet of who I am—in the same way that his once being a character in one of your books is only one part of who he is."

"I create good characters, but trust me, all three of them are so much more than what I wrote. Before you ask—yes, I think they're safe. It's been well over a year, and none of them has felt any pull to go back through the Veil, and Anne did say it was a one-way trip. Roark worries about Eddy though."

"Why?"

"He thinks he needs to come through and have a full life, not hide behind his computers and my prose. Roark feels a certain responsibility toward all three of them. I wrote the four of them as a kind of four musketeers. Roark is afraid if Eddy doesn't come through soon, he never will, and they might lose the ability to communicate with him."

"Well, I hope he does, then. Eddy does seem drawn to Corinne, and perhaps that will inspire him to come. I'm sure glad Spense did. By the way, thanks for making Spense all kinds of hunky."

It was Sage's turn to laugh. "That wasn't me, girlfriend. That was all Spense, although it sounds like he and Holmes are well hung."

"Not only that, but the man knows how to use it. I've always enjoyed sex, but nothing like the last two nights with Spense."

"I know," said Sage. "When I have readers talk about their book boyfriend and how perfect he would be, I just smile."

"Do you want to help me get this salve packed up so I can take it back to the Savoy?"

"No problem. Do you think you'll sell your farm in Ireland?" The ladies grabbed a box, and began to carefully slide the mason jars into place for transport to the Savoy.

"No. That place is part of my ancestry. It's in my DNA. I'm kind of thinking I'll leave it as is and let one of my neighbors lease the grazing grounds in exchange for taking care of it for me. Everything in there had been handed down and added to little-by-little over hundreds of years. It might be nice to start over fresh."

"If you want, maybe you could make an offer to buy some of the things that are already at Rachel's or Watson's for that matter. I don't know that either Rachel or Gabe is overly attached to anything—except maybe Gabe to that sword—so it might be helpful for both of you. Do you have a bunch of other things you need to do today?"

Saoirse shook her head. "Nothing of any import or that has a time attached to it."

"Good. Then I'm going to co-opt you. Why don't we call the Savoy and see if they can send a car? I have keys to Watson's place. We can have the driver drop us off at Watson's and then take this stuff back. Maybe come back and take us past some of the places Roark has mentioned. Actually, there's only one place I'd be interested in—maybe two."

"In the city, I hope."

"Absolutely. Trust me, you will never get Roark to leave London as his primary residence."

"I think that would be a fun way to spend the day, but I hate to impose on Spense."

Sage laughed. "I may be a writer in residence at

the hotel but trust me—what we pay in rent covers the use of all the amenities, including a car and driver."

Sage called and arranged for the car, and the two of them met the driver just as he pulled up. He loaded the box onto the front seat so he could keep an eye on it and then whisked them off to Soho, agreeing to meet them in an hour.

As the ladies were riding up in the converted freight elevator to Watson's apartment, Saoirse realized how much she hadn't noticed about the building. It was located right in the heart of things. Restaurants, pubs, shopping—all were within easy walking distance. There was even a kind of upscale market where artisans sold their wares—breads, jams, home goods. That might be something to investigate, especially if she and Spense were living here.

"I've always loved Watson's place," said Sage.

"Yes, I'm surprised it's as nicely put-together as it is."

Sage laughed. "That's because he had an interior designer do most of the work. Don't get me wrong; he worked closely with him, and truth to tell, Watson was a bit of a control freak. Did you know Anne is the only woman he's ever brought here? To sleep with, I mean. He's had the lot of us over on more than one occasion, but it's always been a place he kept for himself until Anne."

Saoirse believed it. "I like that he's on the top floor."

"Yes, the upper windows all along one end can be opened, and he has a skylight in the bath, which gives it so much light. I like how the designer mixed a lot of industrial, masculine accents with a more laidback, casual kind of elegance."

As Sage opened the door, Saoirse asked, "Where do you think he got *Courechouse*?"

"What?"

"The sword over the fireplace." She pointed toward the ancient blade, hanging proudly in its place. "Rachel said that when she tried to take it out of the holder, she couldn't move the damn thing, but that it practically jumped into his hand."

"I don't know. But Roark thinks there's more to that story than Watson has let on."

Saoirse nodded. "I agree." She looked around, impressed. "I just realized I've never seen this place during the day. It's so full of light. And this funny little nook would be perfect for me to store all my stuff. I'm a girl with lots of stuff."

Sage laughed. "I know what you mean. Roark is right; we either need to find a place to live other than the Savoy, or I need to sell a shit ton of stuff. I keep thinking I'll miss my house there, but I don't."

"Where is it? On the coast, right?"

A kind of dreamy look came over Sage's face. "It's on the windward side of the Outer Banks in North

Carolina. I have an almost 270-degree view of the Atlantic Ocean. But London is home now, and I love it here."

"Maybe Anne and Gabe could buy it if it's close enough to where he needs to be for the business."

"That's not a bad idea. It's a pain in the ass to get anywhere by car, but I have acreage so they could build a landing strip or a helipad. I know Gabe is a competent pilot for either fixed wing or choppers, and they could easily do an amphibious plane."

"What the hell is an amphibious plane?"

"See, this is the kind of useless shit you know as a writer." She chuckled. "An amphibious plane is one that has floats on its landing gear so you can land on water, but it also has wheels so you can land on a hard surface."

"If he decides to go, maybe you should talk to him about it. From your description and the few pictures I've seen, it's gorgeous."

Sage nodded. "It is. The one thing I really miss about it—well, two things—are how private it is and the glass atrium I had made into my office. It was so amazing to write in there—during the day, but especially at night. I could look up and see all the stars."

Saoirse smiled. "That sounds lovely." She strolled into the large, well-appointed kitchen, admiring how tidy and practical it was. I didn't know Gabe cooked," she said.

"He doesn't. But he knew for resale he needed a

killer kitchen. I love the fact that he has that huge fridge. You don't see many full-size fridges on this side of the pond, especially here in the city."

"I am kind of surprised at how big everything is."

"That's because he converted it from a two bedroom, two bath to an enormous one bedroom, one-and-a-half bath. I think he said he knocked out most of the interior walls so he could have larger primary spaces—kitchen, bedroom and living room. I also love these French doors. The designer found them in France and convinced Gabe to get them."

"They're gorgeous. In fact, the whole place is really beautiful. I can't get over how quiet it is and how much light he has."

They wandered into the bedroom and then into the full bath, which had no tub, but had a shower that looked like you'd need a degree in computer programming to operate it. There was an electronic control panel on the outside of the shower that allowed you to program water temperature, strength of water being sprayed by which shower head, a steam setting and other components of what one thought might make the perfect shower. There were buttons and text screens. Saoirse shook her head and stared in awe.

"I really had kind of settled on Rachel's place in my mind," she said, "but this is amazing. I'm sure it's a lot more expensive, but there's so much room."

"I'm going to admit to having an ulterior motive," Sage admitted. "I know Corinne has been thinking about talking to Rachel. She hates where she lives, and Rachel's flat is just a hop, skip and a jump from the Savoy. And it is much closer to Trafalgar Square, which is really important to her."

Saoirse looked at Sage, intrigued. "I can see wanting to be closer to the Savoy, as she works there. But why Trafalgar Square?"

"I have no idea. Have you ever noticed? She's a little bit of an odd duck. Don't get me wrong, I like her a lot, but there's just something different about her…"

At that, Saoirse couldn't stifle her amusement. "Says the woman who married her very own storybook hero."

CHAPTER 14

*B*y the time they'd finished taking a good look at Gabe and Anne's place, it was time to meet the driver and they headed down to the street.

Once they were in the car, the driver said, "Where are you ladies off to now?"

"Do you know where DSI Holmes lives?"

"I do indeed."

"How about you just drive us by there? I don't think Saoirse has ever seen it. Then, if you'll drive us to the Creswell Mews, I'd appreciate it."

"Yes, ma'am."

They drove to Chelsea past the posh townhouses. The driver slowed and parked in front of one of the end units. The Georgian townhouse had a commanding view of the Thames and a stately manner.

"Gorgeous," said Saoirse.

"It is. Let's see if the four of us *miscreants*, as Roark calls us, can't meet here for lunch. The place is gorgeous, but not stuffy. Rachel just loves the place."

"I can see why. So, what's in the Cresswell Mews?"

"For one thing, the former home of a famous author is for sale."

"Oh my God, that would be so perfect for you!"

"I think Roark knows that alone would be tempting for me. My agent wants me to start thinking about moving to more mainstream novels. She thinks that while erotic is big right now, she's afraid the pendulum will swing back the other way. My books will still have sex in them, but the plot would be more intricate and more of a focus. I've always had, according to my old publisher, too much plot for an erotic novel. But you know what? I found those were the ones my core readers really loved."

As the weather was so lovely, Saoirse felt tempted to enjoy it to the fullest. "Do you want to just walk to the mews?" she asked.

"That's a great idea."

After arranging with the driver to pick them up in two hours outside the Creswell Mews, they began walking to their next destination. The sun felt delicious on Saoirse's skin.

"Should we call the agent to see if we can get in?" she wondered aloud.

"No. I'm not ready for that. I just want to wander in the mews itself and see how it feels."

"You love living at the Savoy."

"I do, but Roark is right. Part of it is that I'm afraid something might happen if we leave the hotel for too long…"

"I don't know that I wouldn't feel the same. For me, it's easier as Spense has always lived away from the hotel."

"Exactly. And as Roark points out, I promised myself a long time ago not to make decisions based in fear."

Saoirse reached out and squeezed her friend's arm gently. "But risking Roark—mind you, I don't think you are—that would give me pause if it was Spense, and I haven't been with him very long."

"Roark is everything to me. I could lose all the rest, but as long as I had him, I'd be fine."

Trying to lighten the mood, Saoirse said, "Duh. You did write him based on your own fantasies."

Sage laughed. "So he likes to remind me when he's slapping my ass for something I've done."

"I know. I don't get it. I used to try to tell myself there was something very wrong with me."

"Me too. But then I think you get to a point where you just accept it. But when you find a man who truly understands what it is you need and enjoys providing it, it's wonderful. Spense is a member at Baker Street. They're going to be sorry to lose him as a training

Dom. Both he and Holmes were kind of their go-to guys. In fact, the last time I talked to JJ, she was saying it's hard to keep a good one because they inevitably find someone and then step down."

"Is that kind of weird—to go to a club where people are walking around naked?"

"Not everyone is naked and not all clubs are the same. But in any event, especially at Baker Street, there's a kind of freedom. JJ Fitzwallace makes very sure that no *mean girls* become members. She is the undisputed queen of the place, and she wants it to be a really accepting, supportive place for everyone involved. The fun thing is, you can watch and find out different things you want to try. And if you don't want others watching, they have a bunch of private rooms."

"I'm not so sure I want to watch Spense ogling naked women."

"That's the best part. You won't notice, because you'll be ogling all the half-naked, bare-chested guys in leathers. If you think Spense is sexy in or out of a suit? Wait until you see him in his leathers. He is positively drool-worthy… and Watson literally stops conversations."

"And what does Roark say when you're making goo-goo eyes at some Dom who isn't him?" said Saoirse, laughing.

"I don't do it unless he does it first. Then I remind him what is sauce for the goose is sauce for the gander. And then he snarls but doesn't look anymore... and neither do I."

"But can't you watch other people?"

"Sure. Some do actual instructional demonstrations. Try and catch Rhiannon and Sawyer or Fitz and JJ—talk about a palpable connection, and some folks get off on being watched. Interestingly, Anne has a strong exhibitionist streak and Gabe loves showing her off. Roark is just the opposite. I don't think I'd mind, but he can get downright growly so we only play in private—although his hands have been known to wander if we're watching... I think mostly to make me focus on him or give him a reason to spank me—what we call a funishment."

"Okay, now I'm starting to get intrigued."

"It really is fun, and Baker Street is a great place to play. It's a beautiful, very stylish club. There are two mews for sale in the same neighborhood. One is much bigger, but I'm not sure I want bigger."

When they arrived, a lovely young woman dressed casually, but professionally, approached them. "Ms. Mathews? I'm Helen Anderson. I am probably your biggest fan. I got a call from your husband that you might be interested in seeing both of the properties that are available."

"How did Roark know?" asked Saoirse.

"The driver ratted us out. I've pointed out to Roark that if we leave the Savoy, he won't be able to keep tabs on me as easily." Sage shook Helen's outstretched hand. "I don't have fans, Helen. I have readers."

The grin on Helen's face belied her stylish demeanor. At that moment, she was just one of Sage's readers. "I've heard you say that. Would you like to see inside?"

Sage hesitated.

"Come on, Sage," said Saoirse. "We're here. Helen came all this way. At least she can tell your husband we looked."

"You just want to see inside," Sage protested with a smile.

"I do. I'd love to see the one that belonged to someone famous."

"Do you have a preference for where we start?" asked Helen. "We're standing in front of the larger property—there's a little blue plaque that indicates that. If you decide on this one, I'd have another plaque made saying it belonged to you as well."

Helen opened the door and stepped back, allowing them to enter. Neither Sage nor Saoirse could prevent the oohs and ahhs that came out of their mouths.

"This is gorgeous, Sage, and not at all what I expected."

Sage shook her head. "Me neither. I don't know what it was I was anticipating, but this large, light and bright space isn't it."

"And both are close to Rachel…"

"And not too far from Soho, either."

"True, but sad to think Anne wouldn't be here."

"I agree, but remember, Corinne might be interested in Rachel's flat. And I'm not sure where Mazie lives."

"Mazie works for Gabe, right? She's the one who drew the sketch?" Sage nodded as Saoirse continued, "Do you really think Eddy is interested in Corinne? Spense does."

"So does Roark, but he thinks that like you and Spense, Eddy's kind of dancing around it. Oh my God, look at this kitchen! For this kitchen, I'd actually learn how to cook. If you're here in London, you could teach me. Rachel says she's never had anything she didn't love at your table. What do you think?"

"For me, I'd use part of the living room for a nice dining area, get rid of the peninsula, extend the cabinetry and put in an island. I'd also get a nice large fridge like Gabe's."

They headed up the stairs from the ground floor to the first floor and explored the three bedrooms and one-and-a-half baths. And then headed up to the second floor to see the final bedroom and full bath. This was the area the author had used for her writing.

"This is beautiful," said Sage.

Saoirse nodded. "I'd pull up the carpeting and see if the original floors are still there, but if not, I'd put in something similar to the downstairs or some kind of hard surface floor. Can you see yourself writing up here?"

"Unfortunately, I can. I can imagine all kinds of things in this place."

"The one thing the other place has over this one," said Helen, "is that it hasn't been renovated in a long time, so it is pretty much a blank slate. Yes, it is substantially smaller, but the bones are there, and it could be stunning. Would you like to see it?"

Sage shook her head. "No. If my husband is going to tempt me out of the Savoy, this is the one I want."

"It's amazing, Sage, and could be really perfect for you," said Saoirse.

"I suppose you have my husband on speed dial?" Sage asked, eyeing the agent.

Helen grinned. "No ma'am, but I do have his number in my contact list."

"Then get him on the phone and tell him to come down here so we can write an offer. Can we do that here?"

"Absolutely. I have the forms in my car. I can go get them while we wait for your husband. Would you like to just stay here?"

"Won't the owners mind?"

"No. They've already moved out and we had the place staged, so if there are things you like, we can write an offer to include them."

After Helen left them alone, Sage turned to Saoirse. "I'm pretty damn sure one of those bedrooms will become our own private dungeon, and I think I might want it up on that top floor, completely separate and private."

"You naughty girl!" Saoirse laughed as they moved back to the sitting room and sat down.

Sage looked around the room. "It really is gorgeous, but there are only a couple of things that are here that I'd like. This is going to cost Roark."

It didn't take long for Roark to join them.

"I can get back to the Savoy on my own," said Saoirse.

"I don't think this will take too long. Spense said he was almost done for the day. I suggested we go to one of the pubs close by to celebrate. If it is amendable with you, he's going to change into something more casual and will join us. Then we can go back to the hotel to talk to Eddy."

"Sounds like fun."

Saoirse didn't envy the sellers of the property. Roark had done his homework and knew not only precisely what it was worth, but what being able to pay for it in cash within thirty days would mean to the sellers. He wasn't wrong. It didn't take them long to hammer out a deal.

While Roark negotiated, Sage took Saoirse aside to make a preliminary list of things she wanted to purchase for the home.

"Just like that, you leave Roark to hammer out the deal?"

"Yes. I hate that kind of financial crap. Frankly, the bankers and all the other money people are much happier dealing with Roark than they are me. He can drive a hard bargain, but he's fair and at least he cares and knows what they're talking about. Unless the check is going to bounce, I don't want to be bothered."

Saoirse shook her head. "Then that's another good reason you have him."

"I used to do it, but I hated it. For Roark, it's second nature and he knows that by taking that off me, he's helping me focus on other things. Part of the D/s dynamic for us is playing to our strengths."

"I'm beginning to see that. Spense was all pissed off about the encounter with Gull—not because I challenged the doctor, but because I didn't let him keep me safe while I was doing it. The more I thought about that, the more I kind of liked it."

"A lot of people think submissives are fragile or that we exchange our weakness for the Doms' strength. But it doesn't work that way. It can't. If both parties aren't strong, it sets up an imbalance, not an exchange of power."

"I'd never thought about it that way, but I can see where you're right. And honestly, the best three relationships I've ever seen are yours, Anne's and Rachel's… and I've known Rachel a long, long time."

Business concluded, Roark escorted both Sage and Saoirse back to The Lion's Den, a pub close to the Savoy. They didn't have to wait too long before Spense joined them.

Sliding into the booth, he wrapped Saoirse in his arms and kissed her soundly.

"Congratulations on the new home. I talked to Watson and Holmes. Anne and Watson are coming back tomorrow. Holmes and Rachel will join us as soon as they can."

"Something's happened, hasn't it?" asked Saoirse.

"Yes, sweetheart, but it's fine. I just think we're better off to talk to Eddy away from the hotel." When she, Sage and Roark all continued to look at him, Spense sighed. "Dr. Gull paid me a visit, and he isn't happy with us."

CHAPTER 15

*E*arlier in the Day
Savoy Hotel
London, England

Spense shook his head as Sage and Saoirse left the hotel. *There goes trouble.* He went through his daily routine, musing on how much he loved working at the hotel, but admitting to himself that if Saoirse couldn't be happy in London, he'd find something he loved just as much in Ireland.

At lunch, he grabbed something from one of the bars in the hotel and took it back to his office. He hated to be away from the hotel in case a staff member needed him. On the other hand, he liked to be able to eat in peace and quiet. His compromise was to take meals in his office with the door closed. Staff knew if it was important, they could interrupt him, but he trusted them not to bother him unless it was absolutely necessary.

His cock throbbed against the front of his trousers. It didn't give a damn about staff or food. It very much wanted to be bothered by Saoirse and allow her to soothe its ire by being deep inside her where it would do them both a world of good.

Saoirse had proven to be every bit as passionate and responsive as he'd ever dreamed she might be… in fact, more so. Each time he reached for her, she was soft and warm and ready to receive him. He delighted in making her wait for his cock. His Saoirse was a woman who liked having his dick up inside her, thrusting in and out, pleasuring them both. And pleasure him she did.

He was just taking the last bite of his sandwich when a sudden chill seemed to settle over the room. Spense pushed back from his desk and waited…

Nothing happened.

"Alice?" he said softly. The room began to shake. "Not Alice," he said to himself.

"You and your witch are interfering in things which do not concern you," said Gull as he materialized in front of him.

"Tell me something, Doctor…" The doctor's eyes widened, indicating his surprise. "Yes, we know who you are, Dr. Gull, and we know who Alice is and what you did to her and those you threw away with her, you sick bastard. But my question is, can those outside hear you speaking, or do I sound like I'm talking to myself?"

"No one can hear us."

"Good to know."

"Do not meddle in things that are far beyond your comprehension," said the doctor in a haughty tone.

"The souls of five girls trapped in my hotel *are* my concern," Spense insisted. "I suggest you set them free. If you try to interfere, you will find yourself in a world of hurt. My lady is a witch, but two of my friends and I are not of this world, and the other member of our group is a combat veteran and one of the toughest sonsofbitches I've ever known. Come to think of it, my other two friends are not the only ones who are as tough. You might want to think long and hard about trying to fight us. So far, we're three and zip against supernatural beings. I rather imagine either Azrael or the banshees would like to drag your ass to Hell. If I were you, Dr. Gull, I would leave this hotel and those girls alone. Otherwise, I will unleash my beloved on you. That is an encounter you will not survive."

"Those girls are not important," said the doctor.

"They are to me and my friends. We'll find them…"

"They are of no consequence."

"No, the secret you're trying to protect has no importance. You're trying to preserve the reputation of Prince Albert Victor…"

The doctor cackled—an ugly sound. "You know nothing. His reputation was in tatters long before his sorry end. Her Majesty and her legacy are what's important. I did what needed to be done to protect Her Majesty and the Realm."

"More and more of what Queen Victoria was really like is coming to light, so whatever you think you can hide, you can't. We have a friend who can track down the most minute facts that will lead us to the girls and to what your queen's part was in that tragedy."

An evil smile lifted the corner of Dr. Gull's lips. "Your friend Eddy can be dealt with. Do not think his pitiful non-existence will save him."

Spense tried to hide his own reaction; he had to get word to Eddy.

"I think you'll find Eddy much harder to kill than you think. One stroke of his keyboard and he'll erase you out of existence," said Spense, hoping he sounded a whole lot more confident about that than he felt. "I'm telling you, Doc—walk away and find a place to hide. Maybe, just maybe, we won't come after you."

The room shook violently again, and then Spense was left with what remained of his lunch and the growing belief that they were most likely going to need help. He pulled out his personal laptop and signed onto the message center where they communicated with Eddy.

Spense: Eddy, Gull is on to you. Take care. Will contact you tonight away from the hotel.

Eddy: Message received. Staying off the Savoy system. Even piggybacked is probably a bad idea.

Spense closed up his system and walked to the front desk. "I need to go grab something for later. I may be a few minutes late getting back," he said.

"No problem, Spense. We'll hold the fort down," said Tami, a long-time employee of the hotel.

He left the building, crossed the street and walked along the Thames, dialing first Holmes, who agreed they'd get off at the next port and be back in London as soon as possible, and then Watson.

"Damn it, Spense; this had better be good," snarled Watson on the other end of the call.

"Oh, I don't know," said Spense. "You tell me. The little girl in the yellow Victorian dress that haunts the fifth floor? We think she and four other girls were raped trying to cure Prince Albert Victor of syphilis. The quack that facilitated that, one of Queen Victoria's physicians, decided to trap their souls somewhere in the hotel. Once we started looking for them, Dr. Gull began showing up and threatening everybody. Good enough?"

For a moment, there was quiet on the other end of the line. Then… "Yeah. We'll check out in the morning and head back to London unless you need us tonight. And sorry about the bad temper. I should have known you wouldn't have called unless it was important."

"And I'm sorry I had to call. Tomorrow morning is good enough. Would you mind if we met at your place? I think if we're at the Savoy, Gull can hear us."

"No problem. Sage has a key."

"We'll see you then. My apologies to Anne."

Spense could hear the scuffle for the phone.

"Spense? It's Anne. Do you think the bodies are there in the Savoy?"

"It makes sense as Alice seems trapped here, but I know every inch of this hotel. If the remains of five little girls were here, I'd know it."

"Not necessarily. The hotel was built over what was left of the Savoy Palace, which was destroyed in 1381 during the Peasant's Revolt…"

"I'm aware of the history of the site…"

"Yes, but as I doubt you've ever lived in a castle or a palace—ouch, Gabriel that hurt." Spense could hear mumbling. "I'm sorry, Spense, if it sounded like I was getting on my royal high horse. I wasn't. I was being practical. If you, or anyone else, have not lived in a castle or a palace of that era, you might not be aware of a very popular feature known as an oubliette. It's a kind of hellish dungeon where people were thrown to die a slow, lingering death. If he salted the bodies after they were dead and then again when he tossed them down the oubliette, it could keep their spirits from rising, especially if they did not die in a state of grace."

"Those children did nothing wrong," said Spense, trying to hold his temper.

"You and I know that," said Anne gently, "but my guess is *they* didn't. And whoever did this to them probably made sure they thought it was their fault. The mind can be a powerful thing."

Spense shook his head, even though she couldn't see him. "I think, Milady, you may well have given us a large hand up on this. I owe you my thanks… and again, my apologies."

"None are necessary, Spense. We'll see you tomorrow."

Spense: Eddy, check to see if the Savoy Palace had an oubliette. If so, see if you can find the most likely place for it to be here in the hotel.

Eddy: I'll see what I can do.

Roark was just exiting the hotel as Spense returned.

"I think my beloved has seen the light about a new residence—not that we won't miss everyone here," said Roark.

"Understandable. The double Mews house?"

"I believe so. It'll probably take a while to get the deal done. Why don't we meet at The Lion's Den? When I've got the place bought, we'll go there and wait for you, and we can all have dinner together to celebrate."

"Sounds good. I'll see if I can't wrap things up here sooner rather than later."

"Are you all right? You look a bit on edge."

"I am, but it's nothing that won't wait. I'll see all of you later."

∼

"Gull? When? Where?" said Saoirse, running her hands over what she could get to in an attempt to make sure he was all right.

"I'm fine, sweetheart…" he said, pleased that she seemed so concerned.

"Would you tell me if you weren't?"

"Yes. I was having lunch in my office when Gull showed up doing the room shaking thing again. He seemed quite perturbed that we had figured out not only who he was, but what he had done. And he was never trying to protect the prince. He did what he did in what he thought was service to the queen."

"It doesn't matter why he did it; what he did was unconscionable," said Sage with a shiver as Roark put his arm around her.

"Agreed. When I spoke to Anne, she reminded me that the hotel was built on the site of a palace that was destroyed in the fourteenth century. She said to look for something called an oubliette and suggested that if Gull had convinced the girls they had not died in a state of grace, they might have trapped themselves."

"Bastard," hissed Saoirse under her breath. "And if he salted the oubliette, their souls would not have been able to ascend. I'll bet you anything that's what he did."

"How do we counter that?" asked Roark.

"Either use salt that was blessed by whoever blessed the salt he used to curse those girls or—you are so not going to like this—we grind up a bone of the person who cursed them and sprinkle that bone dust, which will contain sodium or salt to counteract the salt he used."

Sage took out her phone, and within moments looked up and said, "Anyone fancy a trip to Essex? Specifically, to the St. Michael Churchyard Thorpe-le-Soken, Tendring District?" She shook her head and snorted. "Seriously? His gravestone talks about doing what the Lord requires but to do it justly and to love mercy. Does that asshat really think that if he escapes an eternity in the Void, he'll get to go into the Light?"

"Probably. He convinced himself that sacrificing those five girls and condemning their souls to never rest was done in pious service to the queen," said Saoirse.

"That's exactly what he said to me. That what he did was never for the prince, but for Queen and Country."

"Let me get this straight," said Roark. "Are you three talking about grave robbing?"

"Yes, but more importantly, we're talking about

freeing those little girls and allowing them to finally rest in peace," said Sage.

"I understand your reservation," said Saoirse, "but there's no other way. If we do it right, the only one who will ever know will be Dr. Gull, and if I have my way, he'll be in Hell and it won't much matter what he thinks."

"Should we ask Eddy to search for an oubliette within the Savoy?" asked Sage. "Wait, does Gull know about Eddy? Is he safe?"

"As safe as any of us until we get rid of Gull, but I did give Eddy a heads-up. We're going to try and keep our communication with him outside of the hotel. We're going to head to Watson and Anne's place to talk to him."

"Speaking of which," said Roark, "Gabe hasn't made a final decision, but I think he and Anne may be headed back to America."

"His old unit?" said Spense. Roark nodded. "It must mean they've found the other swords."

"What other swords?" asked Saoirse.

Spense continued. "Gabe and the three men in his unit who survived were charged to find the other three legendary swords from the Knights of the Round Table. *Courechouse* was the first and was given to Gabe. The men agreed that once they found the others, they would form a kind of security team that could be hired to help those who needed them."

"A kind of mercenaries with honor," said Roark,

with just a hint of sarcasm. He looked at Spense. "Are you really on board with grave robbing?"

Spense nodded. "I don't give a damn about Gull or his eternal rest, and if Saoirse says we need some bone dust, then I say we go get it."

"Good God," said Roark. "Well, if the lot of you are going to jail, I'd best go with you."

CHAPTER 16

They finished eating, stopped by a market to pick up a few things for the evening at Gabe's, and then went back to the flat in Soho.

Riding up in the lift, Spense remarked, "I've always liked this place."

"If Watson takes Anne to America, he might be willing to sell this place to us," suggested Saoirse.

Roark laughed. "I do believe if you'd suggested the two of you purchase a yurt in outer Mongolia, Spense would be happy as long as you see a future with him."

"Don't pay any attention to Roark. I don't even want to know what he had to give for their new Mews house."

"The agent suggested Sage get another blue plaque to put underneath it to say it was hers as well."

"I think those things are an official designation" Sage replied. "Not sure we can do that…"

"But you're happy, aren't you, love?" said Roark.

"Yes, but you really don't fight fair. How am I as a writer supposed to turn down the opportunity to live in the same house as a great mystery novelist?" said Sage.

"You aren't. I think that was the point," said Spense.

"It just kind of feels like we're all breaking up…" said Sage.

Roark wrapped his arms around her. "Life is all about change, love. Nothing ever stays the same, but friends like ours don't have to remain in one place. Those ties that bind us will keep us eternally bound one to another."

"He's right," said Saoirse. "Look at Rachel and me. Even when she was in America and I was in Ireland, we might not get to see each other as often as we do now, but it didn't lessen our friendship in any way."

"I've got an idea," said Spense. "What if we all agree to meet every year at the Savoy on New Year's Eve or some other day? We'll all make a commitment to gather together at least once a year at the place that brought us all together."

Sage brightened almost immediately and kissed Spense's cheek. "I think that's a marvelous idea. It'll be hardest on Gabe and Anne…"

"Right now, but who's to say? I might decide that yurt in outer Mongolia is just the place," teased Saoirse.

They all laughed as they headed into Gabe and Anne's Soho flat.

Roark and Sage hooked Spense's laptop up to Gabe's system so they could project the computer screen up onto his television while Saoirse and Spense set up food. Saoirse went through the contents of the fridge, making sure that nothing had spoiled, and then prepared a pot of Irish stew that could simmer in the slow cooker and easily be kept warm until they arrived. Saoirse had also picked up some good, crusty bread.

"I don't think Gabe or Anne expects you to go to all of this trouble," said Spense.

"Sweetheart, I can make stew with my eyes closed. I figure they'll be hungry when they get back, and we might be as well. That's why I wanted to hit the market."

"We talked about Rachel's place; this one would be more money."

"I know, but it's a lot bigger and there's an upscale market with stalls to rent where I could set up a place to sell handmade candles, soaps and various things. I think it could help my business grow."

"Let's talk to Gabe and Rachel and crunch the numbers. But if we can swing it, I'd like this place as well. I wouldn't be unhappy at Rachel's…"

"I wouldn't either, but the kitchen in here is bigger, and that little niche would be perfect for a lot of my ingredients."

"You two about ready? It's almost six-thirty," said Roark.

"Ready," Saoirse and Spense said in unison as they joined Roark and Sage in the sitting room.

The TV monitor showed interference and then blipped on and they could see his face. Eddy was a lean, muscular man, with dark angular features, a thick head of almost black hair and a perpetual shadow.

Eddy:I'm so glad to see all of you. Our friend Dr. Gull has been busy. It was fortuitous that Spense gave me a heads-up. I was able to ensure he hasn't figured out the internet. Just to be safe, I blocked him out of certain areas so that he's kept away from sensitive information and the dark web.

Sage:It's so good to finally see you. You look just like I described.

Eddy:I am most grateful that you didn't see fit to describe me as you did our poor friend Spense. I am sure his lovely lady feels the same. Spense, how did you manage that? You look nothing like Hercule Poirot.

Spense:I have no idea, but I'm ever so grateful—and stop flirting with Saoirse.

Eddy:But I am French. I flirt with all the beautiful women.

Spense:Not mine.

Eddy:Mademoiselle Saoirse, please tell me he lies.

Saoirse:I'm afraid not.

Eddy:Then I shall remain eternally heartbroken.

Spense:Knock it off, Eddy.

Eddy:I am wounded, my old friend. You know me well enough to know I would never try to take what is so obviously yours.

Saoirse:Good God, Sage, did you write all of them to be this obnoxious?

Sage:No. Eddy was always supposed to be a minor character for humorous relief.

Eddy:Again, I am wounded.

Roark:Might I remind the lot of you that some murderous Victorian physician has his sights set on us? Eddy, Watson and Holmes are on their way. Watson should be here later tonight and Holmes within a day or two.

Eddy:Can I assume that Watson is now aware of who and what we are, or were in your case?

Spense:You can. And are you aware that his wife is…

Eddy:The beautiful Anne Boleyn. Bravo to her for getting her own happily-ever-after. I am sorry they are having to cut their honeymoons short, but I think it is important that you try to stick together. I wouldn't advise anyone being on their own. I know Dr. Gull paid Spense a visit earlier today…

Spense: Saoirse believes she knows a way to counteract the curse and set those girls' spirits free.

Eddy: *Bien!* That takes care of half your problem, and I had no doubt the talented Irish witch could handle that. It is Gull himself that you must get rid of before you free those poor children.

Saoirse: Any idea how we do that?

Eddy: I am researching that now, but any ideas of where I might look would be helpful.

Saoirse: I'll try doing some research.

Eddy: How do you plan to break the curse?

Roark: Trust me when I tell you, you don't want to know.

Eddy: *Mes amies,* I would suggest that you not allow your beautiful ladies to go without you. Now, onto the good news. I have found the oubliette. The bad news is it will be difficult to reach. I am attaching a file that shows the rough drawings of the Savoy Palace and how it relates to the placement of the hotel. I can give you an approximation but finding it may prove complicated. And as I'm sure you have figured out, your Dr. Gull is not a good man, although in his defense he truly believed what he did was for the good of the country.

Saoirse: Helping some depraved prince with syphilis rape little girls is a crime with no justification whatsoever…

Sage: And then to murder them and then deny

them their eternal rest? I'm with Saoirse; there is nothing that justifies what they did.

Eddy:Spense, I took the liberty of giving you a few days off. It is backdated, and everyone will think it was always that way. I don't think any of you should go back to the hotel until we are ready to deal with Dr. Gull.

Sage:Some of us will need clothes…

Saoirse:And even though they're locked up, I have two spell books I'm going to need.

Spense:Then I suggest we go as a group tomorrow, grab what we need and get out.

Roark: I'll call Holmes and bring him up to speed. My guess is he'll invite us to stay at his home. It's large enough to accommodate all eight of us. We'll work out the logistics on this end. Anything else?

Eddy:No. I'll keep looking for a way to rid the world of Gull's malevolent spirit. *Bon chance* to us all.

The screen blipped off

"I don't know about anyone else, but I'm feeling the momentous weight of all of this. Saoirse, why don't you and Spense bed down here? Watson and Anne won't be here until sometime tomorrow. If you have the key to Rachel's, we'll head over there and meet back here in the morning," said Roark.

"Sounds good to me. Call when you leave Rachel's, and I'll make sure we have something for breakfast."

"Take care of each other and be safe," said Sage.

"You too," said Spense, kissing her on the cheek and walking to the elevator with them. Once back inside, he closed and locked the door and engaged the alarm system. "I'm not sure that's going to work on a vengeful ghost."

"I'm not sure Gull is a strong enough spirit to leave the place he's tied to."

"Wouldn't he be tied to the place he died?"

Saoirse shook her head. "Not always. Sometimes it's to the place where your life was the most impacted. For example, Catherine Howard was executed on Tower Green, and yet she is said to haunt one of the hallways at Hampton Court. That's where she broke away from her guards and ran down the hallway screaming for Henry to grant her mercy. It's said it was then that she knew there would be no reprieve. She was buried in an unmarked grave and continues to try to get Henry to treat her with mercy. Anne says Catherine was a fool to ever think having pricked his ego, he would let her live."

Spense chuckled. "Do you ever find our lives rather odd?"

"Not really. I was born and raised a witch. I have always believed in the supernatural. Anne was born more than five centuries ago and waited until she could pierce the Veil and create her own happily-ever-after. And you, Roark and Holmes used to exist only in Sage's books. Only Watson and Sage don't have some kind of paranormal side to you. Trust me when

I tell you, as long as she has Roark, she couldn't care less about any of it."

"Any ideas about Gull?"

"You mean how to get rid of him? Not a clue."

"Do you think you could get the banshees to help?"

"Doubtful. For one thing, I think Gull is tied to the site of his final infamy. For another, it isn't a good idea to ask the banshees for help too often, and I think someone might notice them coming screaming out of the heavens to drag Gull down to Hell."

"Yes, Roark said it was quite impressive. In fact, he said it was the single most terrifying thing he'd ever seen. He warned me that any man who wanted to be with you would need to understand that you were capable of wielding great power."

"Did that worry you?"

"Yes and no. I wasn't in the least bit worried about my feelings for you, but I did wonder if I had enough to offer you. I'm just a hotel concierge. Granted, I'm the head concierge and I supervise all of the front desk, valet—what in the restaurant world they call the front of the house—staff in the greatest hotel ever built, but still I'm not a famous private investigator, or a DSI with Scotland Yard or starting up some kind of supernatural protection service."

Wrapping her arms around his neck and nestling her body against his, she said, "And I'm not a famous and wealthy novelist, or the former Queen of

England come back to life, or a historian who forged a new life for herself and helped to send Jack the Ripper to Hell…"

"No. You're just the amazing witch who has worked tirelessly to help Anne fit in and was the one who actually called on the banshees to take the Ripper where he belonged."

"And you're the man who loves me knowing full well how crazy my life can be—the man who in a very short time has made me feel safe and loved and cherished. I don't know, Spense; I'm beginning to believe we're going to be just fine."

"More than fine, Saoirse. I believe Roark came through the Veil to save Sage; Holmes to save Rachel. Perhaps I'm the man who came through the Veil to protect you so you could work your magick."

"Make love to me, Spense. I need to fly free, safe in your arms."

"With pleasure," he all but purred as he swept her up in his arms and carried her into the bedroom.

CHAPTER 17

They took their time getting naked, lazily undressing one another—kissing and stroking exposed skin. Spense laid her down on the bed, with her legs hanging over the end, spreading her legs as he knelt before her. Leaning down, he kissed down from her belly button to her sex, using his tongue and lips to seduce her. If Saoirse needed him to show her his devotion, he was fine with that. He would worship her every day for the rest of his life.

Parting her labia, he inhaled the scent of her arousal and smiled. He hadn't done anything, yet she was soft, wet and ready for him. This was the way it was with them. Neither had to do anything at all for the other one to be ready and wanting. And his Saoirse wanted him—of that, he was sure.

As he covered her sex with his mouth, his tongue speared her. She cried out, running her fingers through his hair. He nibbled, licked, sucked and stroked her using only his mouth, lips, teeth and tongue. Saoirse writhed beneath his oral onslaught. The sighs and moans became whimpers of need, calling to his cock, which throbbed in rhythm with her cries of pleasure. He was hard and he needed to be up inside her, shoved deep. But for now, he would feast on her.

He moved his mouth up to her clit, which peeked out from its hood. As he slid one long finger inside her pussy, he swirled his tongue all around her little jewel before sucking it into his mouth, causing her to tremble.

"Spense, please," she said breathlessly.

He continued to stroke her wet heat with his finger, watching the way her body responded. He settled his mouth over her clit and began to suckle, working his mouth and finger to bring her to orgasm. It wasn't difficult. Saoirse's body had already learned the pleasure it could expect from his. Her body arched up and she gasped as she climaxed, her response coating his hand.

Spense rolled back up onto his feet and stared down at her warm, sated body. He felt as though he were some kind of god, and this woman before him was the sacrifice being laid at his feet. But he had no intention of killing her. No, he would join with her, and together the two of them would be greater than either would have been without the other.

His beautiful Irish witch was a glorious sight. The bed had cocoa-colored sheets, which set off Saoirse's pale blonde hair. She opened her eyes; her pupils dilated with desire. She smiled, and like the wanton creature she was, she reached for him, inviting him to join with her in the most primal and definitive of ways—male to female, yin to yang, light to dark, positive to negative. They had been drawn together from the first time they'd met, and yet they had taken their time to come to know each other.

"Scoot up on the bed," he commanded softly and she complied.

Saoirse understood there was a part of him that needed to be in control and had figured out that by gifting him with her submission, she held a power in their relationship that he would never deny. Spense crawled up on the bed, settling his body on hers as she wrapped her legs around his trim waist.

Spense thrust in hard, spearing her until he was balls deep, establishing the connection he felt each time he fucked her. Saoirse climaxed again, just from his possession. He had come to expect that. He could work his way into her tight pussy to tease her, but his Saoirse gloried in being possessed by him and when he took her in a less finessed manner, her body responded accordingly—her pussy clamping down on him.

"God, yes," he crooned as he dragged himself back and then drove deep again.

"Yes," she purred like a tigress.

He had planned to make long, slow love to her, but his need was too great. He'd torture her that way in round two. For this first time tonight, he allowed the dominant male that resided in his soul to take over. Again and again he hammered her, driving them both toward the edge of the abyss. As he felt her pussy tighten around his cock, he pounded into her, until he felt the sizzle run down his spine and he thrust hard and deep, grinding himself against her as he gave up his cum and flooded her sheath with all that he had.

"I love you, Felix Spenser," she whispered as he rolled from her body and onto his back, pulling her up against him and holding her close.

"I'm glad to hear that because I feel the same way about you."

He would have said something more, but Saoirse was out like a light. Not knowing how to deal with Gull must be taking its toll on his beautiful witch, he decided. But they would figure it out. Together, they would deal with the deadly Dr. Gull and see his soul consigned to Hell.

∽

"Oh I like that… I get called back from my honeymoon and come home to find you messing up my sheets," said Watson, dropping their bags just inside the bedroom.

"Gabriel, be nice," chided Anne.

"Nice ended when my honeymoon got cut short."

"Really?" Anne said, drawing herself up. "How is what we were doing in Paris any different than what we were doing here?"

Saoirse loved watching the two of them. Whenever Anne was annoyed or upset, she defaulted to her Queen of England pose, which never impressed Watson.

"If you two are going to put on a show," Saoirse retorted, "you could at least have brought popcorn."

Gabe laughed. "I'd tell your boyfriend there to spank you for that sassy mouth, but I do believe I smell Irish stew coming from the kitchen."

"I'm surprised he ever uses his brain," said Anne. "Generally, he's either thinking with his cock or his stomach."

"Watch it, your Majesty. You're on thin ice with me as it is."

"What could I have done? We were on public transportation the whole time." She grinned at Saoirse. "That bullet train was so much fun. I never knew anything could move that fast."

"I suppose that wasn't your hand under the blanket playing with my cock?"

"I just wanted to make sure my most valued possession was safeguarded."

Gabe shook his head. "Out, Anne. Let's let

Saoirse and Spense get dressed. Where's the rest of the gang?"

"Holmes and Rachel are waiting to dock and will then fly home. Sage and Roark stayed at Rachel's last night."

"Has Victoria become a problem?" asked Watson.

"Quite the contrary. Her name is Alice Moore, and she and four other little girls all under the age of thirteen were raped and murdered."

Anne gasped. "Don't tell me diseased men still think they can cure themselves by raping virgins?"

"That's bullshit," said Watson.

"It was bullshit in my time too, but it didn't stop them."

"Mostly it is no longer believed, but they died during the reign of Queen Victoria," explained Saoirse.

"That hypocritical bat? And I thought Catherine of Aragon was bad," said Anne.

Saoirse suppressed a grin. Anne had very definite opinions concerning the monarchs of England—most of them not overly kind except where Elizabeth I and Elizabeth II were concerned. She admired both Queens for putting aside their own happiness to rule, protect and serve their country.

"But the doctor who did it trapped their souls inside an oubliette that was part of the Savoy Palace. Eddy has defined the area where it might be…"

Anne nodded. "If I can see drawings of where he

thinks it could be, I might be able to narrow it down. The palace was gone before my time, but I've seen more than my share of oubliettes."

Spense's cell vibrated, and he picked it up. "It's a text from Sage. I told them you're back and to come join us. Saoirse said she'd feed everyone. Now get out, so we can get dressed."

Anne and Gabe withdrew to the sitting room. Saoirse and Spense got up, showered together and dressed. Saoirse headed into the kitchen while Spense stripped the bed.

"Anne, you said you wanted to learn to cook," said Saoirse. "I feel a bit weird inviting you into your own kitchen."

"No, I want to learn. I figure we can't eat out at restaurants for the rest of our lives, and while my gorgeous husband is a god in the sack, he can't boil water to save his life." Gabe's hand connected with her ass and the former Queen of England jumped and giggled.

"Maybe not, but I can heat that sexy ass of yours up pretty damn quick if you're not careful."

Gabe headed into the bedroom to help Spense.

"This physician has you worried," said Anne, who seemed at times to understand her better than anyone save Spense.

"Yes. I haven't a clue how to deal with him. I think we've figured out how to free the girls, but Gull has made it clear he will try and fight us. He's an evil man."

"How did he trap them?" Anne asked.

For Anne, belief in Saoirse's power came easily. People in the Tudor era believed in magick and witches, so it wasn't something she questioned.

"I think he salted their graves."

"Can you get blessed salt nowadays?"

"No, but if I can get at his bones, I can grind them into dust, which will release the salt in them. And that should counteract the salt he used."

"Grave robbing?" Anne said, grinning. "Count me in."

Gabe walked in. "Seriously?" He turned to Spense. "You signed off on this?"

Spense shrugged his shoulders. "I'm not the one who was raised and trained as a witch. If Saoirse say's it's the only way to save those girls, we're going to have to do it."

"Do you think you can raise him from his grave or will we have to dig him up?" asked Anne, obviously excited about the prospect.

"I've got news for you, my beautiful wife. You are not digging up, raising up or anything else around a grave. Jesus, Anne, what if you all get caught?"

Before Saoirse could reply, Anne leveled him with a look. She was good at that.

"I might point out to you that we had a massive sword fight with a specter and the Angel of Death on the lawn of the Tower of London, and no one saw a thing. I'm pretty damn sure Saoirse can handle it." Anne sensed she was pushing Gabe too hard and joined him, wrapping her arms around him. "Saoirse knows what she's doing. If she says she can get these bones without anyone knowing, she can. Can't you, Saoirse?"

"I think so. One of the things I need to do is to make sure the grave doesn't look disturbed. I want Gull gone, but I don't want to upset any of his descendants. They had nothing to do with what he did."

"For what it's worth, Gabe, Saoirse hasn't said how many she'll need to go with her. We're trying to stay away from the hotel, and we wired Eddy up through your system. I hope you don't mind."

"As long as Saoirse's cooking, stay as long as you like. We can take turns using the bed."

Anne rolled her eyes. "No, we can't. I have no intention of either missing out or having to be worried about how much noise I make."

Gabe started to laugh in spite of himself. "You know, baby, for a woman who had her head cut off, you're awfully easy to love."

Gabe drew her into his arms and kissed her. There was a brief knock on the door before Roark and Sage joined them. Anne and Sage joined Saoirse in the kitchen, while the men withdrew toward the back of the flat.

"How dangerous is this doctor?" asked Gabe.

"As a spirit? We're not really sure. He's shaken a couple of floors around him, but Saoirse can do the same. Unless Eddy comes up with something from the dark web, I don't think we have any other option than to follow Saoirse's lead."

"Agreed," said Roark. "I don't particularly like the girls being in the line of fire, but I don't think we can do this without Saoirse. Trying to keep Anne, Sage and Rachel out of it will be more work than it's worth, as I don't think we'll be able to do it."

"Well then, step one is to get the doctor's bones and let Saoirse grind them into dust so she gets the salt from them. And I agree with Anne; I don't think there's much chance in getting caught doing that. What I don't want is to try and free those girls unless we have some kind of plan to deal with Gull."

Both Roark and Gabe nodded in agreement.

"I talked to Holmes this morning. They should be here tonight, and they are more than amenable with all of us staying at their place," said Roark.

"We'll be fine here," said Gabe.

"Eddy said he thought there was some safety in numbers. Gull is pretty much confined to the hotel at this point, but there's no saying if that will hold true once we start to move against him," said Spense.

"Holmes gave me the code to a hidden lock box,

so I can get us in and we can get settled. I think that's our next order of business after breakfast. And I have no idea what Saoirse is making, but it smells marvelous."

"I've never been a big breakfast eater," said Gabe. "I may just have some of that stew."

"I can attest to how good her stew is," said Roark. "Sage says Saoirse loves to cook, which makes this a better flat."

Roark left them to join the women.

Watson shot a look of curiosity at Spense. "What did he mean by that?"

"I'm afraid in all the craziness, Roark disclosed your plans to move to America."

"Ah. We were going to tell everyone. I just talked it over with Anne. I made a vow to those guys a long time ago and frankly, I'd feel more comfortable with an ocean between her and the Tower of London."

Spense nodded. "I can't say I blame you. But if you're going, what are you going to do with this flat? Saoirse and I are planning to move in together, and we think it would be ideal."

"Let me talk to Anne, but that would be great. It would certainly make it easier for us," said Gabe, catching Anne's eye and smiling as he and Spense wandered back toward the kitchen.

"Where do you think you'll base out of in the States?"

"We want to be on the East Coast but haven't

decided on anything specific." Gabe ran his hands through his hair. "We're not sure of any of the details, just know that the time has come to fulfill our destiny, as Ben likes to say."

"Gabe?" Sage beckoned him with the spoon she was using to serve food. "Have you thought about the Outer Banks of North Carolina? You're a hop, skip and a jump from Atlanta, Norfolk, Richmond and Charlotte, and just a bit further to D.C."

"That's gorgeous country," said Gabe, nodding.

"I know someone who has a gorgeous place that they're thinking of selling," Sage said with a grin. "Roark and I are never going to live there. Maybe you and Anne should buy it. There's a private dock and plenty of room for an airstrip and helipad."

Anne joined them. "Breakfast is almost ready and if Sage is offering to sell us her place, I say we go for it. It's huge and we could set up the company to run out of there. The others could find places close by, and like Sage said, it's easy access. All of you fly, and doesn't one of the other guys fly chippers…?"

"Choppers," Gabe corrected.

Anne grinned, and Spense wondered if she hadn't made the goof on purpose. Anne was good for Gabe. He could occasionally brood, and Anne seemed to be able to alleviate some of the worry that seemed to plague him. He wondered if the shadow he'd often seen clouding his friend's face hadn't had something to do with whatever it was that had happened in

Gabe's past that had triggered him and his former comrades into making a vow to one another and to a greater cause.

"Choppers. I've seen pictures of the land and house, and it's really beautiful. Please, Gabe, can we at least think about it?"

He pulled her close and kissed her. "Anything you want, Anne. I know how hard this is going to be on you. If you think being in Sage's old home will make it easier, we'll see if we can't make it work."

"All right, everyone, breakfast is served."

The six friends grabbed plates and began to serve themselves, pushing away the danger of what was to come and enjoying the camaraderie they shared.

CHAPTER 18

After breakfast, all three couples headed back to the Savoy. Spense, Anne and Gabe planned to go scout out the area that Eddy had indicated might have the oubliette. Roark was to stay with Sage and Saoirse; first, they'd pack for Roark and Sage, and then they'd clean out Saoirse's room so she could check out.

"Maybe Saoirse should have come instead of Anne. She's the one with the magickal powers," said Gabe.

"You are about as subtle as a freight truck," said Anne.

"Train. Freight train, and I'm right about Saoirse."

"Yes, but I have far more experience with oubliettes and I'm the one with the most experience with spirits and things on the other side of the Veil. I'll be fine, Gabriel. I have two proud and noble warriors; Dr. Gull had better be on his best behavior."

"Gabe, if you want, we can take Anne upstairs so you and I can look," said Spense.

Anne snorted. "This bogey man has got you two spooked. What he did to those little girls is reprehensible, but I'm not afraid of him."

They wandered the basement until they found a spot where the temperature was much colder than the surrounding area. Anne walked gingerly and seemed to be in a faraway place.

"They're here," she said quietly. "I can feel them." She shivered. "I can feel him too."

No sooner had the words left her mouth than Dr. Gull materialized in front of them.

"Be gone," he snarled.

"Fuck off," intoned Anne, whose forward movement was halted by Gabe.

The ghostly figure glared at her, eyes full of malevolence. "You are a disgraced Queen, beheaded for treason," he sneered.

"And you are a malingering evil, doomed never to rest for what you did to those poor children," said Anne heatedly.

Gabe's face grew hard. "My wife's only disgrace was that she allowed men like you to control and abuse her. Her own father and uncle betrayed her, and a man who vowed to love her forever had her murdered so he could fuck someone else."

Anne laid her hand on top of his. "It's all right, Gabriel. If all that came before is the price I paid to be with you, I would pay it again. I love you."

Gabe smiled. "I love you too, babe."

Then he moved her behind him in order to shield her from Gull. Spense moved up to stand beside him. If the doctor wanted a shot at Anne, he would have to go through the two of them.

"This is not your business," snarled Gull. "It is before your time and long past hers. I chose to forsake my eternal reward in order to safeguard Her Majesty's secrets."

"You managed to evade the forces of darkness, which would have damned your soul to Hell for what you and your accomplices did, allowing the prince to rape children in a vain attempt to cure himself of a social disease. Then you murdered them, tossed them into the oubliette and salted their graves to keep their souls from rising," accused Anne.

The spirit's eyes widened, and his eyebrows raised, shocked at what they had learned. "Go away. You cannot help them, and I will do all that is within my power to keep you from thwarting my purpose."

"Thwart this, you decomposed piece of shit," called Saoirse from behind the doctor.

"Witch," he hissed.

"You got that right, asshole," Saoirse said as she formed a sphere of white light and pushed it toward Gull with great force. The doctor staggered back before the energy dissipated, passing through the doctor before he smiled and dematerialized. Saoirse shook her head. "That's not good."

"Why?" asked Spense.

"That energy ball should have flattened and weakened him. It shouldn't have gone right through him."

"Maybe you're just tired," suggested Spense.

"I am, but it shouldn't have had that effect on something as simple as an energy surge. But it did confirm something I was worried about," said Saoirse.

"What's that?" said Sage as she joined them.

"He doesn't have enough corporeal substance for me to fight. It's one of the reasons I couldn't just kill the Ripper. I'm a witch; I need something of substance to work any kind of powerful magick. I can make a room shake or back him off, but I can't banish him to Hell."

"So, are we back to the banshees?" asked Spense.

"No. Like I said, he's tied to this place, and I can't summon the banshees and ask them to come screaming down in their chariot to drag him away. Don't worry, Spense, I'll figure it out. I have to." Saoirse looked to Anne. "Are they here?"

Anne nodded. "I think so."

"Alice? Alice? It's Saoirse and my friends. Are you here?"

Nothing but silence answered her question.

"We're ready to go," said Roark, leading the group back toward the elevator.

The elevator was small, holding only three adults at any single time. Roark, Sage and Gabe stepped onto the lift. Gabe didn't so much step as get shoved by Anne who didn't give him time to turn around and get off the elevator before the doors closed.

"Alice? I need you to stand where I can see you above the hole he threw you in," entreated Saoirse.

"Please, Alice," added Anne. "We only want to help."

Nothing. They turned to go.

"He won't let you do this," said Alice quietly as her image gained substance.

"We won't let him stop us. You've been visiting me since I was your age. I think we've found a way to free you and your friends. We'll only have one shot at it, so make them ready. Tomorrow when Big Ben strikes midnight, you will feel his curse lift and you will be able to ascend to Heaven."

"We've been here so long…" said Alice.

"I know, but you just need to hang on a little while longer," said Anne. "Saoirse is a powerful witch, and she and our friends have defeated evil before. We will not fail you."

Alice said nothing and then sank back into the earth.

"I hope you're right about that," said Saoirse.

"I know I am," said Anne.

The elevator returned and Spense escorted the two women aboard with a smile.

"What's the smile for?" Saoirse asked him.

"Just thinking that I am escorting a former Queen of England and a witch, who is the love of my life onto an elevator so we can save the souls of some innocents. And here I thought leaving the pages of a book would be the most exciting thing I ever did."

Anne smiled. "I'm so glad you two are together. I think we're moving to America. I'm not sure Gabe will ever be comfortable with us living in London. Besides, I think he has a destiny with those men from his old unit and the swords they possess."

"Do they really believe the swords once belonged to the Knights of the Round Table?" asked Spense.

"Yes, and they were charged with the powers of light and darkness, and the men who wielded them were supposed to use them to protect the innocents of this world," said Anne a bit grimly before shaking it off. "You two should really think about our place. I know you talked about Rachel's, but Gabe thinks that both Mazie and Corinne want it. And the loft in Soho really would be ideal for the two of you."

Spense looked at Saoirse, who nodded. "We agree. After we set those little girls free, we should all sit down and talk."

As soon as the doors opened, Gabe snatched Anne out of the elevator and into his arms. "That's five. Damn it, Anne."

Anne said nothing but stood on her tiptoes and kissed him. "I'm sorry, Gabe. I shouldn't have shoved you onto the lift."

"No, you shouldn't have. Roark has the car loaded, and we're all going to head over to Holmes and Rachel's place."

"I do have an idea of how to deal with Gull, but I'm not sure anyone's going to like it," said Anne avoiding meeting Gabe's eyes.

"If it involves a certain Angel of Death being allowed to claim Gull, you're right. I don't like it," agreed Gabe with a scowl.

"Azrael will jump at the chance to get Gull," Anne argued.

"But we have the same problem with him as we have with Gull—he's tied to the hotel and Azrael can't leave the Tower," said Spense.

"Not as a spirit…"

"No way," said Saoirse vehemently. "I am not bringing Azrael into the world."

"Oh, he's not so bad if you understand him," Anne argued. "He's a greedy bastard…"

"What the hell would he spend money on?" asked Saoirse, momentarily confused.

"Doesn't matter. It's not happening. Anne, you and I have had this discussion. You are forbidden to go within a thousand feet of the Tower," growled Gabe.

Ignoring Gabe, Anne answered Saoirse. "Not

money—souls."

"What are you suggesting, Anne?" asked Spense. "I will not be a party to you disobeying Gabe."

"But if Anne is right…"

"No, Saoirse. And you will not come between them either, lest you find yourself disciplined as well," stated Spense.

They filed into the car. Saoirse's deep, inner concentration concerned Spense. Once at the Holmes townhouse, the other three couples filed out and were surprised when Rachel rushed out to embrace her friends.

"Holmes rented a plane. We thought it was imperative we get home. Gentlemen, why don't you join Holmes out on the patio in the back? I'll take the girls up to your rooms, and we'll get you all settled."

Not really knowing how not to follow Rachel's instructions, but fairly sure they were being played, the men went through the house to the expansive courtyard at the back.

~

As they entered the first of the guest bedrooms, Saoirse turned on Anne. "I won't do it."

"Won't do what?" asked Sage.

"You know I'm right," Anne insisted. "Gull is too powerful for you, but to leave the Tower, Azrael and the Warder will both have to be corporeal. It has to be done."

"Now the Warder? Anne, have you forgotten they were both willing to kill Watson and Holmes to drag you into the Dark?"

"No, I haven't forgotten," said Anne. "In some ways, I think Azrael will be mollified if he gets Gull—you know, kind of a substitution—Gull for me."

"Why the Warder?" asked Saoirse, trying to understand her friend's reasoning but remaining skeptical that either specter—the Warder or Azrael—could be trusted.

"Most recent history notwithstanding, he was always kind to me," Anne said. "I think giving him the chance to guide those little girls to the Light will give him great peace. It's worth a try… isn't it?"

"Those girls are already frightened. Maybe the Warder can help," suggested Sage.

"I believe you can do this, Saoirse" said Rachel. "You've wanted to help Alice for as long as I can remember."

"I'd have to get their word of honor and ensure that the spell has a failsafe so that they're banished back to the Tower regardless of what happens. The timing…" said Saoirse as she began to weigh the odds on trusting either the Warder or Azrael against condemning Gull and helping Alice and her friends.

"Will be difficult," finished Anne. "You'll need to

make the Warder and Azrael corporeal while someone else spreads the salt."

"Salt?" questioned Rachel.

"Long story, but I think it means we're going grave robbing in Essex," said Sage, her eyes dancing.

"The boys aren't going to like that," said Rachel. "And Holmes is already unhappy that we came home early."

Realizing she had no real choice, Saoirse said, "Then let's not tell them. We can sneak out and take the train. We'll be there in an hour."

"How do we keep from being seen and extract the salt?" asked Anne.

Saoirse smiled. "That's the easiest part of this whole thing. I can cast an invisibility spell, and so long as there's no one actually at the graveyard, I can extract a bone without moving any of the ground. When we get back, we can crush the bone. We don't have to separate the salt from the rest of the minerals in the bone. We'll have to coordinate tomorrow night…"

"I think we need to talk to the Warder and Azrael tonight. I have to tell you, I think we need the boys with us at that point," said Rachel.

"We are so screwed," said Saoirse. "After we sneak out and go rob a grave, we're going to ask them to go back to the Tower and deal with the Warder and Azrael. Do we know how to have a fun couples' night or what?"

The other three women laughed. Quietly, they made their way out of the house, calling for a cab to take them to the train station. By the time they arrived, their tickets had been purchased and they barely made the train.

As the train pulled away from the platform, Saoirse looked out to see Spense glaring at her. "Screwed," she said, sitting back.

CHAPTER 19

They sped through the English countryside and arrived at the train station in Thorpe-le-Soken in the Tendring District of Essex. It was a charming little village, and finding St. Michael's church and its cemetery proved far easier than any of the four women who had embarked upon this quest had imagined it might be.

Not wanting to call attention to themselves and wanting to ensure the graveyard was as deserted as it seemed, the four women split up as they entered the burial ground and wandered around.

"Found him," called Rachel quietly.

Looking down, Saoirse said, "The guy had a real sense of irony. Considering what he did, his gravestone talks about *mercy*? What a crock. Anne? Sage? Can you two get about ten yards away from us, diagonally opposite each other, and keep an eye out?

Rachel, I need you with me inside the spell, keeping an eye on them. This is going to take some focus on my part, and it'll help not to have to be watching."

"Of course I'll do as you ask, but why?" asked Sage. "Aren't you going to be invisible?"

"Yes, but just because what's happening within the bubble of the spell can't be seen, it doesn't mean that we aren't here. Someone could bump into us, which could be difficult to explain. If you can give us a heads-up, we might be able to move out of the way."

"That makes some sense," said Anne.

Once everyone was in place, Saoirse began to cast the invisibility spell. Having her three accomplices present allowed her to focus on the work itself. While the invisibility spell was not terribly difficult, exhuming a portion of bone from the doctor's grave without disturbing it was going to be far more taxing.

As it always did, the spell to become unseen made the things within the bubble of the casting soft and a bit unfocused. Within that somewhat fuzzy vision, she now had to sharpen her focus in order to reach into Gull's grave with her magick, break off a piece of bone and remove it from his casket. She wanted to retrieve a substantial enough piece so that when it was crushed, it would render enough salt to counteract what Gull had used to damn the souls of those little girls to that dark pit.

Thinking about what he had done angered Saoirse, which took away from the energy she could put into the two spells. Working one kind of magick within the confines of another was not an easy thing, and twice she had to start the removal over. Finally, she was able to separate a piece of the radius bone in Gull's arm.

She was bringing the bone up through the grave when Rachel touched her shoulder. "We aren't alone."

Even that brief lack of concentration caused her to lose the focus needed for the most delicate part of the combined spell. Swearing, Saoirse looked up to see a man and woman entering the cemetery. Glancing at Anne and Sage, she could see that they were studiously attending to the graves of those that they were standing closest to, and to the casual observer looked to have nothing to do with one another.

"I'm going to try again. Keep an eye on those two people. Let me know if we need to move."

Once again, Saoirse focused her energy on seeing the bone in her mind's eye and raising it up from the depths of Gull's grave. Slowly the bone began to ascend. Dematerializing it within his coffin and then reconstituting it once it was removed would have been easier. It might also have resulted in losing some of the density of the bone, meaning they wouldn't be able to extract enough salt to free the girls.

Finally there was a small disturbance of the earth, and the bone broke free. Saoirse removed the silk cloth she'd brought with her and used it to pick up and then wrap the bone.

"They left. We're in the clear," said Rachel, who understood the need for calm and quiet where spells of this nature were concerned, even if she didn't wield magick herself.

Saoirse rose slowly to her feet and allowed the walls of invisibility to fade away.

Anne was shaking her head and smiling as she said, "That was amazing."

Feeling weakened, Saoirse reached for Rachel, who steadied her.

"Not as easy as it looks, is it?" said Sage. "I've thought about doing a series featuring a coven of witches. Would you be my technical consultant? I'd like to get it right, and I don't think a lot of books portray the reality of being able to do what you do."

"I thought I saw a nice place for lunch. Why don't we go there and just rest a bit? We can then either head for Rachel's or wait for our significant others," said Anne with a smile.

"We're going to miss you," said Sage.

Anne nodded. "I feel the same. The three of you are really the only close friends I've ever had. But Gabe isn't comfortable being so close to the Tower, and he does have *Courechouse*. There's a reason it came to him. I truly believe he and his former comrades have a destiny to fulfill with those swords."

"Lighten up, you two," said Saoirse. "It isn't like

it's forever. Rachel, Spense suggested we all get together once a year at the Savoy. And besides, America isn't that far away. It's not like we're living during Anne's time, when it was pretty much a one-way trip unless you lived your life at sea."

"She's right," said Rachel. "And we have so much technology. We could do lunch once a month via zoom or video call."

Anne wrinkled her brow. "Do I even want to know?"

"Think of it as a kind of electronic magick. We won't be in the same room, obviously, but we'll be able to see and talk to each other. And if we're getting together once a year at the Savoy, maybe we could do once a year in America as well," said Sage.

"We'll figure it out," said Rachel. "We don't intend to lose touch."

Saoirse moved so that she stood facing her three closest friends. "I don't know about the rest of you, but I'm a bit like Anne. With the exception of Rachel, I've never had a group of girlfriends that I could trust implicitly. I will not give any of you up. Anne, at one point Rachel lived in America; it didn't matter. We stayed close." She put her hand in front of her, palm down. "I say we vow to do the same."

One-by-one Anne, Rachel and Sage laid their hands one upon the other, saying, "I so swear."

Feeling better about the future and her energy

starting to return, Saoirse said, "Let's go see what this town calls a good place for lunch."

As they were headed toward the café, Sage's phone vibrated with a text.

"I thought we all turned our phones off," said Rachel.

Sage laughed. "That's Roark. When I shut my phone off, he has Eddy turn it back on and ping me. Trust me, they now know where we are. Let me answer this." She quickly typed in a response. "I told him we were all fine, had what we needed, were going to have lunch and be back at Holmes and Rachel's in a couple of hours. He isn't too happy with me, but if I was sure we were safe, they'd see us when we got back."

"Which means," said Saoirse, "that they're up to something themselves."

∽

"Did it work?" asked Spense.

"Yes. Eddy is quite good at enabling me to use Sage's phone as an electronic leash of sorts. Not foolproof, but I can generally keep tabs on her. The girls are having lunch and will be on their way back to London. According to Sage, they *got what they went for*. You lot should thank your lucky stars you aren't married to a romance writer. She does the most annoying things in the name of research…" Roark paused for a moment. "Then again, she does make a lot of money, and there are times I get back to our suite and she attacks me because she's turned herself on."

The other three men chuckled.

"I would point out," said Holmes, "that of the lot of us, yours is the most inclined to behave."

Spense clapped Gabe on the shoulder. "Not to worry, old son. I do believe yours is going to have to relinquish her title as the worst behaved."

"The only problem is, that's not because Anne's going to behave any better... just that Saoirse is a brat of the first order, and I say that with nothing but affection."

"I fear you are right," chuckled Spense.

Holmes turned to Roark. "I must say I'm astounded by all that's happened since Rachel and I got married. Let a man go away for an abbreviated honeymoon, and the lot of you run amok. Roark and Sage buy a home—and a famous one at that—Gabe and Anne decide to move to America, and Felix decides to get his head out of his ass and go by a new moniker. By the way, Spense, I have to agree with Saoirse. Spense is a much better fit. Felix might have worked for the guy described in the book, but thankfully for Saoirse's sake, you don't look a thing like him."

"Have any of you ever wondered why?" asked Gabe. "According to all of you, Roark and Holmes both look like their characters. But you, my friend, are a far cry from Christie's super sleuth. Roark, on another note, Anne and I talked. We'd like to buy the house in North Carolina. That's gorgeous country; it could accommodate the new company, and it's small enough and remote enough to be a good fit for Anne. Didn't Sage say there was an old barn?"

"That's good to hear," Roark said. "I think selling it to friends will make it easier for her. Do me a favor and tell her you can't live without her roadster. I'll pay you to keep it. And yes, there's a barn in good structural condition, but it needs some work. I think there were eight or ten stalls. Do you and Anne like to ride?"

"Yes, my father's parents had a farm outside of Chicago. When he married my mom, he turned his back on that lifestyle, but I loved it. I spent most every summer with them. And Anne loved to ride but was prevented by her family from riding astride or even alone. She was expected to ride pillion, which is behind a man with her legs on one side—sort of sidesaddle without the saddle."

"It sounds like you'll be putting that stable to good use," said Holmes.

"I think so. Anne says she's seen pictures, and the place really calls to her."

"It is beautiful, but our lives now are so caught up here in London. I think it's easier for Sage to adjust to being here than vice versa," said Roark. "Having a house versus living in a hotel will make her feel more settled."

"I thought she loved living at the Savoy," said Spense.

"She does, and your staff spoils her rotten. But when she got divorced and the books became so successful, buying that house and restoring it went a long way to establishing her sense of self and achievement. I think having the Mews house will do the same for her here."

"You should probably get used to the idea of being descended on at least annually," said Holmes. "My guess is, once a year isn't going to be enough. In all honesty, I'm not sure I'd be okay with only seeing you once a year. I've rather enjoyed going to Baker Street and that cigar pub over by Gabe's. And while I know the three of us can still do that, it won't be quite the same without you, Gabe."

"I'm going to miss all of you as well, but I made a vow…"

"Understood," said Spense. "Fate is calling your name. Sage did some research on that sword of yours. If it's called you as its master, then you are needed for something bigger than head of security at the Savoy."

CHAPTER 20

By the time the women exited the train in London, Spense and the others were waiting on the platform. Together, they all headed back to Holmes and Rachel's townhouse. Once there, Saoirse collected her mortar and pestle and headed out into the courtyard.

"Aren't you worried about losing some of the dust to the air outside?" asked Anne.

"Better that than having everyone inside inhale stale bone dust. Regardless of how gently or slowly I grind this into dust, there are going to be particles that hang in the air."

As old and brittle as the bone was, it crushed easily, and it didn't take long for Saoirse to render it into a fine powder that could be easily sprinkled across the oubliette. She secured it into two parts, each nestled in its own plastic cling wrap, ensuring nothing would escape until the right time, and then enclosed each package in its own silk pouch—one larger than the other.

"So, the plan is to sprinkle that on the ground?" asked Roark.

"I'm afraid not," said Saoirse, glancing at Spense. "This is where the plan gets a bit tricky…"

"You mean the grave robbing portion of this plan wasn't the most difficult?" he asked speculatively.

"I wish. A small invisibility spell and extraction, although by no means easy, is relatively straightforward and could have been done by one person. Having Rachel, Anne and Sage made it less stressful for me, as I could focus on the two spells. I don't think for a second Gull is going to just stand idly by and let us release those girls."

When no one contradicted her, she continued on. "We need to dig down to get to the oubliette. We'll need to have it open so that the bone dust can be sprinkled into it, and it can filter down. It'll need to be done slowly and thoroughly so we ensure it covers the entire space."

"I think we can count on the doctor trying to interfere," said Spense. "Digging that opening is going to take a bit of doing. This morning, I had the maintenance staff cut out the concrete to get us down to the dirt. I just heard from them that they were successful. We'll still have to dig down, but at least that part of the flooring is out of the way."

"Did they ask why?"

"Oddly enough, they didn't. But then, I've asked them to do odd things before." Spense turned to Saoirse. "What's the part you don't want to tell us?"

"We have to deal with Gull. I don't think freeing those girls will be the end of him. He needs to be removed from the Void."

"You want to send him to Hell," said Watson.

"I think we might get some help with both that and helping those girls into the Light. The last thing we want is for them to get lost in the Void, and we have no way of knowing if the Light would open a path to them at this point," offered Anne.

"No," said Watson.

Anne took his hands in hers. "I don't think there's any other way."

Gabe looked to Saoirse. "I thought you said the Warder and Azrael couldn't leave the Tower."

Saoirse took a deep breath. "Here comes the tricky part and let me say, if I didn't agree with Anne that we need help to ensure the girls get to the Light and the doctor ends up in the Dark, I wouldn't even consider it. But she has a point. We know Azrael and the Warder."

"But how do we get Alice, her friends and the doctor all to the Tower?" asked Roark.

"We don't," Saoirse said. "We need to make the Warder and Azrael corporeal or corporeal enough that they can travel."

"So you think we unleash Azrael on the world?" asked Holmes in disbelief.

"No," said Spense. "That's what had you looking at those spell books all last night."

"They are more appropriately referred to as Grimoire. And yes. I think I found a spell by my three times removed grandmother that will do the trick and seems fairly straightforward. I'm not as concerned about the Warder. Azrael is the one I don't trust, but that's why I separated the bone dust. The majority is needed to salt the oubliette. The other I will use to bind Azrael to only being able to take the doctor and no one else."

"Before anyone wants to object," said Anne, "I know the Warder and Azrael better than anyone on this plane of existence. I believe the Warder only acted against me as he had no choice. I'm sure he will welcome the opportunity to take those little girls into the Light. But Azrael is every bit as evil as you think. He is also arrogant and believes in what he does. I think he, too, will jump at the chance to drag the doctor into the Dark. Maybe not as good a catch as me, but the doctor, too, has evaded his judgment for more than a century. Azrael will relish the idea of seeing him in Hell."

"It makes sense," said Rachel, her voice dispassionate. "Think about it. Anne does know both of those entities better than any of us, and from a historically religious standpoint, it does have a certain logic.

If Saoirse can bind Azrael to the doctor, then we will have the control we need."

"We're going to need to split our team into two smaller forces," said Spense. "Don't get me wrong, I hate this idea on a myriad of levels, but I don't see we have a choice unless we're ready to abandon those little girls…" When no one argued, he continued. "Much as I dislike this, I think Holmes, Watson, Anne and Saoirse need to go to the Tower. Gabe, I can well imagine your fear…"

"Why can't Anne remain at the Savoy?" Gabe demanded.

"Because if anyone can convince Azrael that exchanging the doctor's soul for mine is a good trade, it's me. I know I can convince the Warder to help the girls. I truly think he's a benevolent spirit and was cursed to his fate. Doing this might even help him."

"She's right, Gabe; you know she is," Spense added. "I don't like the idea of being separated from Saoirse, but she's the only magick wielder we have. And I'll be needed at the hotel to ensure nothing goes amiss or we aren't disturbed. So Roark, Sage, Rachel and I will go there and will be working to dig down to the oubliette."

"What's to stop the doctor from doing something to the lot of you?" asked Holmes.

"The first stop on this evening's tour of fun events is the Savoy. I'll cast a protection spell around a specific area. I'll outline it in chalk. As long as the four of you stay within it, you'll be fine. And when we arrive, we'll have Azrael and the Warder with us."

"I suppose I ought to give the Warder back his halberd," said Holmes.

"Only if he agrees to help us," said Anne, "but yes, I think you should consider that gone."

The four couples spent the remainder of the afternoon preparing to do battle against a malevolent spirit that had kept five little girls from their eternal rest for over a century. Gabe had brought *Courechouse* with him to Holmes' place. They had dinner together, and then everyone went upstairs to change and ready themselves for the ordeal ahead.

Once they were assembled in the foyer, Anne giggled. "I love the fact that we all have the right outfits to do these kinds of things."

That broke the tension, and everyone either smiled or laughed. Anne, Saoirse, Holmes and Watson took Holmes' SUV and headed for the Tower, while Rachel, Sage, Roark and Spense piled into Watson's SUV and headed back to the hotel. They had decided that if anyone saw Watson's SUV pulling into the secure freight area, they were less likely to think anything about it or think something was awry.

Holmes parked his SUV in an obscure area close to the Tower. "Do we offer them a ride?" he asked.

Saoirse smiled. "No. There'll be no need. For the spell to work, they have to agree to becoming corporeal for this task alone, or I pull the plug. I've built safeguards into the spell, but I still need them to agree. Blowing the dust into Azrael's face as soon as it even vaguely resembles a human will put him on the track of the doctor, and he will be eager to seize his prize. The Warder will just drift along behind us."

They walked the short distance between where they parked the SUV and the Tower, making their way down to stand before Traitor's Gate. Saoirse raised her arms to the moon and began to intone:

> "With this fog, I blind from hearing and sight,
> All that doth occur this night."

Over and over, she repeated the spell. The fog and mists of London rose from the surface of the Thames and spread like a shroud over the Tower. As they placed themselves in front of the door to the Queen's House, both Holmes and Watson took a defensive stance—Watson with *Courechouse* and Holmes with the Warder's halberd.

Saoirse turned to Anne. "You're up. If they come when you call to them, that's a pretty good indication that they're willing to play ball."

Anne stood tall and called out in a loud voice. "Anne Boleyn, Queen of England, calls upon the guardians of the Void. To the Warder, I entreat you to come this night to the aid of five young girls' souls who have been lost to the Light."

They waited, holding their breath, until the Warder of the Tower walked through the door.

"Your Majesty, I never thought to see you again," he said, bowing to Anne.

"I hadn't planned on seeing you either. But there are five little girls who were raped and murdered. The man who did it salted their graves so their souls were trapped."

The Warder looked troubled by the news. "I cannot leave the Tower, and there is no way for you to get those poor children to me."

"What if there was a way to free you from the Tower, if only to get the children?"

He bowed his head graciously. "I would go gladly and thank you and your friends for allowing me to do so."

Anne turned to Saoirse. "Good enough?"

"That'll do," replied Saoirse.

"In that case," started Anne.

"I don't like this…" growled Gabe.

"I know, my love, but they've been waiting so long…" Taking a deep breath, Anne called, "Azrael, you are commanded to my presence." When there was no reply, she tried again. "Get your skanky ass down here, you miserable wanker!" She turned to grin at Gabe, who returned the smile in spite of himself.

Coming from deep within the bowels of the Tower, they heard a sound that could only be described as a cross between a wail, a screech and a roar.

Anne glanced at the Warder. "Is he always this melodramatic?"

The Warder tried to hide his amusement, but failed, a grin growing across his face. "I'm afraid the Angel of Death is not used to being summoned."

"Well, unless he wants the banshees to show him up for the miserable, ineffective spirit he is, he'd best get his butt in gear. I am not accustomed to having to wait, and he has until the count of three. One—two..."

"You dare command me to your presence?" asked Azrael as he came through the door, hooded cloak and scythe included, and hovered above the ground.

"I do indeed. You no longer have dominion over me. My beloved husband wields *Courechouse* and can end your existence like this," she said with a snap of her fingers. "Know that the Irish witch has found a malevolent spirit that needs to be dragged into the Dark so that his soul is tormented for eternity. Unlike me, he is guilty of arranging the rape and murder of five innocents and has evaded your justice for more than a century."

The Angel of Death lowered himself to the ground. "And you will deliver him to me?"

"No. That is beyond our ability, but the witch can give you enough corporeal substance so that you can go to him. You will be bound to the retrieval of his black soul—and his alone. Should you try to play us false, you will lose your power and vanish into nothing."

Azrael turned to look at Saoirse. "You can do this?"

"I can and will. It was only Anne's magnanimity that saved you last time." She figured if Anne could make up stuff, so could she. After all, magick always worked better when those involved believed.

"The powers that control you can't be too happy that I got away… and they knew I was innocent," Anne added. "I think it will go a long way towards restoring their faith in you if you deliver this blaggard to Hell after so long."

The Angel of Death seemed to ponder his choice for a moment. Then, his hood bobbed as he nodded in agreement.

"They're all yours," said Anne, stepping closer to Watson.

CHAPTER 21

Saoirse stepped forward, passing the small pouch with the doctor's ground bone to Gabe. She turned first to the Warder and intoned the spell that would give his spirit enough form so that he could move to the Savoy and help Alice and her friends.

He bowed to Saoirse. "I am in your debt and ready to be of service. I caution you about Azrael. He does have his own warped sense of duty, but is not completely trustworthy."

"Not to worry," said Saoirse. "I don't trust either of you."

She turned to Azrael and Watson stepped up behind her, readying the pouch so he could blow the dust into Azrael's face as he took form. Again, Saoirse spoke the words of magick and power, and the Angel of Death began to take shape. She would always be reminded how much he looked like the evil specter in several movies—his skin gray and his face not quite human.

Watson pushed her behind him, shook the bone-dust into his hand and blew it into Azrael's face—or what passed for it. The spirit cried out and then settled, turning toward the Savoy.

"He may not be there if you get there before us, but our friends are readying themselves. If he isn't already trying to stop them, he will when they are finished lifting his curse."

Azrael turned back to her, an evil slash of a smile dissecting his face. "What is to stop me from taking my revenge on them?"

"Because I'm not stupid. There is a powerful spell protecting them from him and you. Step out of line, you bastard, and I won't return you to the Tower; I'll call the banshees down on you and have you sent to Hell—appearances be damned."

The Angel of Death paused and then seemed to acquiesce. "Your wish is my command."

Saoirse snorted. "Only because you have no choice. Now if you two will come with us…"

~

Spense and Roark had worked tirelessly to get down to the trap door that concealed the oubliette. Sage and Rachel helped by moving the dirt and broken wood away from the opening so that they weren't in danger of a cave-in. Finally, they struck the wood of the trap door.

With the first knock, the ghost of Dr. Gull appeared. "You will not do this!" he declared.

Spense climbed out of the hole. Roark secured a strong rope to the ring handle and then Spense helped him up.

"It doesn't matter anymore," said Spense. "What you did was monstrous, but even if it had been necessary or had worked, everyone involved—including you—is dead. It's time to set these children free so they can spend eternity in the Light."

"They do not know the way, and their passage closed a long time ago," said the doctor in an imperious tone.

"I wouldn't be so sure of that," said Spense as he looked to the door.

Anne, Saoirse, Watson and Holmes entered the room. The doctor turned to vent his rage on those outside the protected circle.

"Come on, big guy," said Saoirse, moving away from her companions. "How about you try on someone your own size?"

"Watson, Holmes, Anne—get in here," called Spense as he grasped the halberd still in Holmes' possession. "I'll get Saoirse."

"You are a witch and should have been burned," snarled the doctor.

"You and your kind never figured out that most of those you burned didn't have an ounce of magick in their souls. They were innocents, blamed by the ignorant for things far beyond their control. My kind have always hidden in plain sight, and most were far too powerful to be trapped by the likes of you," Saoirse bantered.

Gull moved toward her, but Spense thrust the halberd into his side, stopping his motion. The doctor didn't bleed, but Spense could feel the substance of the man's spirit impaled on the weapon. He heaved the ghost away from Saoirse.

"Get in the circle," Spense ordered Saoirse.

"I can't. Even my magick won't work within its boundaries, and I have to be free to lift the actual curse so that Alice and her friends can finally be free. I have to make sure this thing works. They've been waiting far too long. Rachel, salt the oubliette."

Dr. Gull screeched and moved toward the circle, bouncing off the spell of protection as if he were a rubber ball thrown against a cinder block wall. Failing to get to those protected by Saoirse's spell, he headed toward Saoirse and Spense.

"You work your magick, sweetheart. I'll keep the old doctor here at bay until our friends get here."

Saoirse nodded as she heard Big Ben striking midnight:

As the Tower bell begins to chime;

***Those that died will rise sublime. For those who fell from grace and did the crime,
Their soul to Hell will be consigned***

When the Warder of the Veil and the Angel of Death floated into the room, Dr. Gull drew back fearfully. He seemed to realize that not only were the children being freed, but now he was trapped and there was no escape for him. The spirits of Alice and three of her friends rose from the depths of the oubliette.

"No! No!" Gull cried, backing away from Azrael, who swung his scythe and sank the sickle through the doctor's midriff, making him scream.

"You will not evade your fate again," the Angel of Death cackled, as the adults within the circle surrounded the ghosts of the four frightened girls. He inclined his head to Anne. "I owe a debt to you and your witch. It would seem, Your Majesty, that fate has finally revealed your true destiny. You were a noble queen, and you deserve to be happy."

Azrael began to lose his substance. "Do not fear, witch, I have released my corporeal form, and my prisoner and I will be returned to the Tower where I will take him into the Dark."

A swift and harsh whirlwind encircled the Angel of Death and Gull, who was screaming in agony and fear at what awaited him.

"Irene was too small," cried Alice. "The salt you sent to lift the curse did not touch her."

Spense turned to the others. "Roark, Holmes, Watson—you grab the rope. Saoirse left a little bit of the dust with me, just in case. Lower me down. I'll free Irene. As soon as I find her bones and sprinkle the salt, I'll call up." He looked at Saoirse. "Can you still free Irene?"

"Why do you think I gave you the last remnants of the salt?" she responded, her eyes showing her acceptance of his support of her magick.

Anchored by the rope his friends held, Spense rappelled down into the oubliette. The stark horror of what had happened here, not just to the children, but to others was almost overwhelming. He looked around. The salt that had been spread twinkled in the dim light.

The small child, Irene, lay flattened against the side of the pit. Spense withdrew the last of what remained of Dr. Gull above ground and sprinkled it liberally over the bones before stepping back.

"Saoirse," he called up, "I found her. I've salted the bones and the surrounding ground." He could hear Saoirse intoning the spell that would lift the curse, allowing the child to be led to her eternal rest. He felt the temperature shift from warm to chilled, and then a lovely little girl with long, dark hair began to emerge. "It's all right, sweetheart. Let yourself rise. Your friends are waiting for you."

"You... you freed us."

"Yes, with a group of my friends, headed up by a

former Queen of England and my beloved Irish witch. Go on now."

"Where will we go?" she asked, frightened.

"There's a very nice man who will lead you to the Light—the place you were always meant to be."

"Will he hurt us like the other?"

Spense could feel a part of his heart break. "No, sweet girl. No one will ever hurt you again. I promise."

That seemed to reassure her, and her spirit began to rise. Once she was halfway up, Spense tugged on the rope and felt his friends begin to draw him toward the top as he climbed his way out.

"Thank you," said the little girl as she joined her friends.

Saoirse swept her hand around and broke the protection spell that encircled them. She turned to the Warder of the Veil. "It's up to you now."

"I will not fail you or these children," he said, bowing his head to her. Straightening his spine, he held his hand out to Alice. "I understand you were the one who put this in motion. You have all been so very brave. Take my hand, and we will go into the Light where you will spend eternity in peace and joy." The Warder turned toward the Tower. "Oh good, I can see your families gathering. They have waited for so long for you to join them. Let's not keep them waiting any longer."

Alice took his hand, and one by one, the

remaining girls took the hand of the girl next to her to form a chain. As the Warder started to go, Holmes stepped in front of him, offering him the halberd.

"I suppose you deserve to get this back," he said.

The Warder shook his head, refusing the offer. "I will leave that in your care. You and your friends have given me a great gift this night, and I will not forget it. My thanks to you all."

He led the girls toward the closed door. Just before she disappeared, Alice turned to look at Saoirse. "Thank you. I knew you would set us free." She followed the Warder through the door, vanishing just before walking through it as did each of those who followed.

"Well," said Roark, clapping his hands together, "now that we've done that, who's for a nightcap and munchies in Sage's and my suite?"

"What about the hole?" asked Sage.

"I thought we'd call the archaeological society and let them know there's a number of bones down there. I saw at least three or four other sets of skeletal remains. We've got all night to come up with some reasons as to how and why we found them," said Spense.

∽

Several hours later, the group dispersed. Sage and Roark stayed at their suite; Watson and Anne returned to their flat; and Spense and Saoirse joined Rachel and Holmes at the latter's townhouse. Exhausted from the part they had played in setting Alice and her friends free, each couple returned to their own rooms.

Saoirse and Spense leisurely undressed each other and crawled into bed.

"Do you think he got them to the Light?" Spense asked her.

"I do. What you did tonight—leaving the circle and then jumping into the oubliette—was stupid and incredibly brave. I now have an inkling of how you must have felt when I confronted Gull. I think you're right about your fate. I think you came through the Veil to protect me." She wrapped her arms around him and rolled to her back, encouraging him to cover her with his body. "I'm awfully glad I am your destiny."

He smiled down at her as his stiffened cock homed in on where it wanted to be. "That's good because they say there's no fighting fate."

"Oh, you can fight it, but the only win is if you surrender to it."

Spense thrust into her with a relentless intensity that took her breath away. There was no foreplay, no preparation—none was needed. Just a single hard push into her, connecting them in a way neither had ever felt before their first joining.

"I love you," she said, knowing that there would

never be another for her. She'd been waiting her whole life for him to step out of a manuscript and become her perfect lover.

~

Thank you for reading *Contract: Masters of the Savoy!* I've got some free bonus content for you! Sign up for my newsletter https://www.subscribepage.com/VIPlist22019. There is a special bonus scene, just for my subscribers. Signing up will also give you access to free books, plus let you hear about sales, exclusive previews and new releases first.

Have you been waiting to see if Eddy is ever going to come out of the pages of Sage's books? Then you'll want to read BOUND. Turn the page for a First Look into Bound.

Masters of the Savoy
Advance
Negotiation
Submission
Contract
Bound
Release

Followed by a First look into an upcoming spin off series Masters of Valor.

If you enjoyed this book we would love if you left

a review, they make a huge difference for indie authors.

As always, my thanks to all of you for reading my books.

Take care of yourselves and each other.

FIRST LOOK - BOUND

Corinne Adler opened one eye as the alarm clock on her dresser went off. It wasn't as if she didn't have an alarm on her phone, but her phone stayed by her bed. The old digital alarm with its annoying beep was across the room so that she had to get up to shut it off. The damn thing continued its obnoxious siren's call to get her ass out of bed. She grabbed one of her pillows and threw it at the dresser, managing to knock over a lamp and a necklace hanger—completely missing the offensive object.

Resigning herself to the inevitability of having to get up, she threw the covers back, swung her legs over the side of the bed and stalked across the room, managing to stub her toe on the end of her bed.

"Shit!" she growled, finally reaching the alarm clock and pressing the reset button... But still it continued to bleat at her. She hit the button a second time; the clock bounced but continued to squawk at her.

Corinne grasped the back of the clock, grabbed the power cord and jerked it out of the wall. Blessed silence. She stumbled into the kitchenette area of her small studio. It was all she'd been able to afford when she was attending college, studying journalism and English. She'd been so proud of herself—the first in her family to have a college degree.

She sliced the supposedly pre-sliced bagel and slid it into the toaster. *Why do they say they're sliced when they aren't?* It popped up just as she got her first cup of coffee. Turning around, she wondered why toasters never toasted anything right on the first try. The second try proved to be perfect, and she slathered the bagel with butter and apricot jam before heading over to her one small window that overlooked the Thames and Trafalgar Square beyond. Lord Nelson stood in his heroic pose, the four Landseer Lions resting at his feet. She slumped down in the chair, watching people crawling all over them, although they weren't supposed to. Smiling into her coffee mug, she wondered what they might do if Big Ben ever struck thirteen times.

The legend was that should the clock strike thirteen, each of the seven-ton statues would come to life and devour the city. Thus, the reason each monarch ensured that there was an entire team in place to safeguard the clock and its workings. But the legends were wrong.

The lions weren't supposed to consume the city, but rather stand with the Sentinel of the Clock Tower to protect it from whatever was trying to come through the Veil. The Landseer Lions were only the most recent representation of the great beasts that protected the city. The Adlers had long been the guardians and masters of the creatures—one child in each generation charged to stand with them if the forces of evil came through the Veil to destroy London.

If the clock struck thirteen, it was a harbinger that something evil was about to make its way into the world through the clock face, which was said to be a window into the Veil—a place where time had no meaning, good and evil were engaged in an eternal battle, and magick ruled. Scary stuff if you were to believe in such things... Luckily for her, Corinne didn't believe such things. Or did she?

∾

Wondering what awaits Gabe and Anne in America? Read PROPHESY the debut novella for the Masters of the Valor series, coming March 3, 2022 turn the page for a first look.

FIRST LOOK - PROPHESY

A MASTERS OF VALOR - NOVELLA

They were once known as Knights of the Round Table, but they had lost the chance to be the defenders of the Light. There were thirteen swords forged for those who sat at King Arthur's table. Now only four remain.

Paris, France
Several Weeks Ago

Gabriel Watson thanked the powers that guided his life for the woman who lay asleep in his arms. He didn't understand all of how she got here, or for that matter how some of his best friends from the Savoy had come into being, and he didn't care. All that mattered was that Anne Hastings, who had once been known as Anne Boleyn lay asleep and replete in his arms. The feeling of absolute joy and satisfaction washed over him.

Earlier that day he'd stood at the end of the aisle as the harp had struck the first notes of Mendelssohn's Wedding March and watched the woman he loved with all his heart and soul walk to him and agree to be his wife. It had occurred to him as he took his vows to her that he'd never planned to marry—much less an older woman, especially one that was almost five centuries his senior, but then so much of his life seemed to have been ruled by happenstance.

Ten years ago, he'd been pinned down by the enemy with his Marine Raider unit. There were four of them: Tristan Crawford, Bennett Greyson, Ford Montgomery and himself. They had pledged their lives and their fortunes to one another as they'd struggled to survive. And they had held to that vow.

But Gabe was a man caught between three secrets, all of which were about to collide. He'd preached to Anne over and over again about the importance of honesty and transparency in a D/s relationship. But he wasn't walking the walk…

"Gabe, what is it?" she whispered, lying next to him.

He'd wanted to find the right time. The text two days ago had pushed his need to tell her from the right time to right now. In the annals of texts sent, it would appear, on the surface, not to be that momentous, but Gabe knew different. It had read: *We've assembled the other swords. Are you with us?* The answer had to be yes, but he'd thought he'd have more time. Time to tell her—to prepare her—that he needed to disrupt their lives completely.

"You need to know I always meant to tell you, but there hasn't been enough time. We swore never to hide things from one another. I need to tell you something I probably should have told you before we got married…"

"Gabe, whatever it is, it'll be fine. Wait, maybe not. If you're about to tell me in another life you were Henry VIII, I swear I will cut your balls off, shove them down your throat and watch you choke on them."

Watson looked down at her incredulously. Even in the dark, he could see her eyes dancing with merriment and the wicked grin he had come to know so well. Leave it to Anne to make him chuckle when he was feeling as though his back was up against the wall. It might well be, but Anne was with him. When he'd faced down two supernatural beings, one of them being the Angel of Death, she'd had to be torn from his side and carried away to safety, kicking and screaming.

"If that's the only thing that's going to be an issue for you, we're good."

"It's the sword, isn't it? *Courechouse.*"

Leave it to Anne's keen intelligence to puzzle it

out—if not the complete story then at least the source.

In answer to his unasked question, she continued, "Your family wasn't there—just the men from your old unit. They need something from you don't they?"

"*Courechouse* and the guys are connected."

"So you knew about the sword before you had to use it... The story you tell about just finding the sword in Cornwall—it isn't the truth is it?"

"No, it's not."

"Tell me," she urged gently.

How had anyone ever thought her to be a scheming seductress? Oh, she was seductive as hell. He routinely, and multiple times a day, fell victim to her innate sensuality and raging libido, but she was also one of the kindest, most loving people he'd ever known. She could be cool and arrogant, as only true royalty could be, but if she cared about you, she did so with her whole heart.

"We were on a recon—reconnaissance..." She still had trouble with some slang, although she'd learned so much, "mission. We'd been sent somewhere we weren't supposed to be. We'd been quasi attached to an Agency mission and if we missed our ride out or got caught, we would be disowned by our government. We were near a place called Sarras in the Middle East."

"The Agency—they're some kind of spy network, right? How could those you'd sworn to serve send you and then distance themselves if you were caught?" she asked.

"Kings and other heads of state have been doing it as far back as conflicts over territory, religion or politics have existed. We knew the risks when we signed on but were convinced we were doing what was needed."

He shook his head and sat up. Anne rested her head on his thigh, her hand on his calf. She had quickly discovered one of the best ways to soothe him was by adopting a more submissive role. There was something about the way she laid her head on his thigh that he found alleviated worry and provided him with a peace he'd only known with her.

Stroking her hair, he continued, "We were pinned down and weren't sure we were going to make it out alive. Our ride out of there had been shot down by a stinger missile—a kind of hand-held, guided explosive device. We saw the chopper explode as he was coming for us. When night fell, the enemy pulled back as we'd made our way onto holy ground—only in our arrogance and ignorance, we didn't know.

We began creeping away from our position, trying to find a way out or at least some place we could take shelter until the next day… maybe even find water. We stumbled—literally—on an old cavern system. We were surprised as it seemed like no one had been there for centuries. There was a pool of clear, cold water. We kept test kits in our pack, and it was drinkable."

"That makes some sense—being in a cave kept it protected."

"Protected," he laughed. "You have no idea, and we didn't care. At the time we didn't know the locals avoided the cavern. We'd run out of water shortly before the sun went down. We knew without it, our chances of survival were pretty much non-existent. We filled our canteens and our extra water pack and then drank from the pool. Nothing ever tasted as good. Well, that's not true. Your pussy is so much better."

Anne slapped at him. "Sometimes, Gabriel, you have no sense of decorum."

"Says the woman who couldn't even wait for us to leave the Savoy after our wedding before having her way with me."

"What can I say? You are most definitely my catnip. Meow."

ABOUT THE AUTHOR

Other books by Delta James: https://www.deltajames.com/

If you're looking for paranormal or contemporary erotic romance, you've found your new favorite author!

Alpha heroes find real love with feisty heroines in Delta James' sinfully sultry romances. Welcome to a world where true love conquers all and good triumphs over evil! Delta's stories are filled with erotic encounters of romance and discipline.

*****

If you're on Facebook, please join my closed group, Delta's Wayward Pack! Don't miss out on the book discussions, giveaways, early teasers and hot men!

https://www.facebook.com/groups/348982795738444

ALSO BY DELTA JAMES

Masters of the Savoy
Advance - https://books2read.com/advance
Negotiation – https://books2read.com/negotiate
Submission - https://books2read.com/submission1
Contract – https://books2read.com/contract1
Bound – https://books2read.com/bound3
Release – https://books2read.com/release-dj

Fated Legacy
Touch of Fate - https://books2read.com/legacytof
Touch of Darkness - https://books2read.com/legacytod
Touch of Light – https://books2read.com/legacytol
Touch of Fire – https://books2read.com/legacyfire
Touch of Ice – https://books2read.com/legacytoi
Touch of Destiny – https://books2read.com/legacydestiny

Syndicate Masters
The Bargain - https://books2read.com/thebargain

Masters of the Deep
Silent Predator - https://books2read.com/silentpredator
Fierce Predator – https://books2read.com/Fiercepredator

Ghost Cat Canyon

Determined - https://books2read.com/ghostcatdetermined

Untamed - https://books2read.com/ghostcatuntamed

Bold - https://books2read.com/ghostcatbold

Fearless - https://books2read.com/ghostcatfearless

Strong - https://books2read.com/ghostcatstrong

Boxset - https://books2read.com/Ghostcatset

Tangled Vines

Corked – https://books2read.com/corked1

Uncorked - https://books2read.com/uncorked

Decanted - https://books2read.com/decanted

Breathe - https://books2read.com/breathe1

Full Bodied - https://books2read.com/fullbodied

Late Harvest - https://books2read.com/lateharvest

Boxset 1 – https://books2read.com/TVbox1

Boxset 2 – https://books2read.com/Tvbox2

Mulled Wine – https://books2read.com/mulledwine

Wild Mustang

Hampton - https://books2read.com/hamptonw

Mac - https://books2read.com/macw

Croft – https://books2read.com/newcroft-dj

Noah - https://books2read.com/newnoah-dj

Thom - https://books2read.com/newthom-dj

Reid - https://books2read.com/newreid-dj

Wayward Mates

Brought to Heel: https://books2read.com/u/m0w9P7

Marked and Mated: https://books2read.com/u/4DRNpO

Mastering His Mate: https://books2read.com/u/bxaYE6

Taking His Mate: https://books2read.com/u/4joarZ

Claimed and Mated: https://books2read.com/u/bPxorY

Claimed and Mastered: https://books2read.com/u/3LRvM0

Hunted and Claimed: https://books2read.com/u/bPQZ6d

Captured and Claimed: https://books2read.com/u/4A5Jk0

Printed in Great Britain
by Amazon